ON THE EDGE

EXTREME LIFE

ON THE EDGE

EXTREME LIFE

By

SIMON KING

CONSCIOUS CARE PUBLISHING PTY LTD

ON THE EDGE
Extreme Life

Copyright © 2018 by Simon King. All rights reserved.

First Published 2018 by: Conscious Care Publishing Pty Ltd
PO Box 776, Rockingham, WA 6968, Australia
Phone: (61+) 1300 814 115   www.consciouscarepublishing.com

First Edition printed August 2018.

Notice of Rights
This book is sold subject to the condition that it shall not, by way of trade or otherwise, be lent, resold, hired out, or otherwise circulated without the publisher's prior consent, in any form of binding or cover, other than that in which it is published, and without a similar condition, including this condition being imposed on the subsequent purchaser. All rights reserved by the publisher. No part of this publication may be reproduced, stored in a retrieval system, or transmitted in any form, or by any means, electronic, digital, mechanical, photocopying, scanning, recorded or otherwise, without the prior written permission of the copyright owner. Requests to the copyright owner should be addressed to Permissions Department, Conscious Care Publishing Pty Ltd, PO Box 776, Rockingham, WA 6968, Australia, Phone: (61+) 1300 814 115 or email: admin@consciouscarepublishing.com

Limits of Liability/Disclaimer of Warranty:
While the publisher and author have used their best efforts in preparing this book, they make no representations or warranties with respect to the accuracy or completeness of the contents of this book and specifically disclaim any implied warranties of merchantability or fitness for a particular purpose. No warranty may be created or extended by sales representatives or written sales materials.   The advice and strategies contained herein may not be suitable for your situation. You should consult with a professional where appropriate. The intent of the author is only to offer information for a general nature. Neither the publisher nor author shall be liable for any loss of profit or any other commercial damages, including but not limited to special, incidental, consequential, or other damages. The author and the publisher assume no responsibility for your actions.

Where photographic images have been provided by the author and people are depicted, such images are being used for illustrative purposes only. Product names may be trademarks or registered trademarks, and are used for identification and explanation without intent to infringe. Conscious Care Publishing publishes in a variety of print and electronic format and by print-on-demand. Some material included with standard print versions of this book may not be included in e-books or in print-on-demand. If this book refers to media such as a CD or DVD that is not included in the version you purchased, you may download this material at www.consciouscarepublishing.com

National Library of Australia Cataloguing-in-Publication entry:
Author: King, Simon 1950-
On The Edge / by Simon King
ISBN 9780648085485 (Paperback)
Rocky Hudson, Editor.

Printed by Lightning Source
Typeset & cover design by Conscious Care Publishing Pty Ltd

ISBN: 978-0-6480854-8-5

DEDICATION

This book is dedicated to everyone who has ever overcome their personal doubts, inhibitions and potential limitations to succeed at confronting the often insurmountable challenges of nature's elements – Air, Water and Earth. It is for those who have challenged the air currents of the atmosphere, who swam, dived, surfed, sailed, rowed, skied, skated, hiked, climbed or in so many other ways overcame their fears, and for those less fortunate who were not as successful in their attempts at extreme recreational pursuits.

Most importantly, the book is dedicated to those people who have grasped less strenuous activities to enjoy and celebrate extremes of life, such as attending community festivals involving unusual and extraordinary subjects, or those that prefer collecting garden gnomes, going to fluoro-parties or appreciating eclectic neon skyscapes.

PREFACE

Our planet has much to offer intrepid adventurers seeking the exhilaration of overcoming Earth's many natural challenges – an unpredictable atmosphere, turbulent rivers/seas/oceans, and extensive formidable terrain. Ideally, they survive the entire process intact.

For those individuals choosing to soar freely through the air almost like a bird, the means for free-falling, gliding or ascending on the winds are considerable, with several innovative techniques having emerged in the late 20th century. The surface and depths of the world's innumerable bodies of water also provide ideal venues for riding wild waters or free-diving deep below the waves unassisted. Introduce the additional thermal element of ice or snow-bound conditions, and the personal challenges of crossing vast tracts of land or water increase immensely.

Even man-made structures, such as seemingly endless and steep outdoor stairs or extensive narrow footbridges across raging rivers or deep ravines, may provide ample personal challenge. However, this book also focuses on the many natural phenomena provided by the climate, oceans and landforms to indicate further extremes that are not necessarily able to be safely challenged.

It is not only humankind pursuing such challenges to their own limits, but also the animals, birds and marine life: some of these species may be reasonably described as actually existing at the 'extremes of life'. A discrete selection of these unique and often extraordinary species contribute an interesting insight into how such life-forms prevail in the natural environment.

This book would not be complete without incorporating other less energetic extreme pursuits. Some people celebrate the extreme by collecting garden gnomes and then even more gnomes, attending community festivals/carnivals convened to honour the unusual and quirky things in life – often in humorous ways – or even by indulging in the sheer artistry and beauty of quality neon signage.

Being 'on the edge' conjures various definitions to many people, but I prefer to think of it as exploring your personal boundaries of endurance or enjoyment without going over that precarious edge.

CONTENTS

LIST OF FIGURES	VI
ON THE EDGE	1
FREE FALL	11
UP AND AWAY	10
AIR AND WATER	19
EXTREME WATER PURSUITS	26
SNOW AND ICE	37
THE SURGING AQUA	45
UNSTABLE ATMOSPHERICS	54
THE LONG HIKE	63
EXTREME ANIMALS	74
CURIOUS AVIANS	85
FEARSOME SWIMMERS	93
FESTIVALS AND OTHER EXTREMES	103
NEON TECHNODREAMS	117
FOOTBRIDGES AND GNOMES	123
OVER THE EDGE	130
REFERENCES	134
BIBLIOGRAPHY	157
ABOUT THE AUTHOR	165

LIST OF FIGURES

Figure 1: The Endless Challenge

Figure 2: Wingsuiting

Figure 3: Ballooning

Figure 4: The Ball Pit Beckons

Figure 5: Cliff Diving

Figure 6: Kiteboarding

Figure 7: Kite Surfer Jumping over Water during Surfing in Red Sea, Eilat, Israel

Figure 8: Whitewater Kayaking

Figure 9: Yet Another Waterfall

Figure 10: Not That Easy

Figure 11: Exhaled Air Bubbles of the Freediver

Figure 12: Chilled Out

Figure 13: Let's Get Started

Figure 14: Riding Powder Snow – I am Flying

Figure 15: Waterspout at Sea

Figure 16: Escape Pass near King Rock, West Kimberley Coast, Australia

Figure 17: Storm

Figure 18: Squall at Sea

Figure 19: One More Bridge to Cross

Figure 20: Rugged Hiking Trail

Figure 21: Staircase beside Devil's Cauldron

Figure 22: Climbing Rock on the Island of Cres, Croatia

Figure 23: The Greater Bilby

Figure 24: The Common Wombat

Figure 25: The Australian Kelpie

Figure 26: The Platypus

Figure 27: Enigmatic Crow

Figure 28: The Blue-Footed Booby

Figure 29: The King Vulture

Figure 30: The Tiger Shark

Figure 31: The Beast Cometh

Figure 32: The Small Fish with Powerful Jaws

Figure 33: Fangtooth Eels are not Sea Snakes

Figure 34: Sesimbra Clown Costume Parade

Figure 35: Clowning Around

Figure 36: Festive Day of Vibrant Colours

Figure 37: Masked People in Kukeri Dance to Scare Evil Spirits, The Surva Festival, Pernik, Bulgaria

Figure 38: *The Blancs Moussis* of Stavelot

Figure 39: The Flying Bird

Figure 40: Eye-Catching Graphics

Figure 41: Let the Party Begin

Figure 42: Wooden Footbridge

Figure 43: Broken Footbridge

Figure 44: Collection of Hand Decorated and Painted Garden Gnomes, Canberra Annual Flower Show, ACT 2008

Figure 45: Surviving the Journey

Figure 46: Start of the Adventure

ON THE EDGE

In the highly challenging world of endurance sporting pursuits, nature provides eager participants with three fundamental elements in which to strive: Air, Water and Earth.

The planet's atmosphere (the Air element) is the source of many unusual meteorological phenomena to assist or hinder such endeavours; ephemeral winds and turbulent air currents, a myriad of severe storms over land and sea, dense fogs, ocean mists and extreme temperatures. The air is also the habitat of many exotic and sometimes unique bird species that could be considered symbolically as extreme forms of wildlife.

The planet's rivers, lakes, seas and oceans (the Water element) provide many more suitable competitive avenues for a person's endurance, such as violent rapids, fearsome waterfalls, towering waves, unpredictable tidal rips, overfalls and whirlpools, and the prevalence of icefields over water and across land. Exotic animals and marine life that co-exist in such aquatic environments also provide a distinctive perspective with respect to these extremes.

Terra firma (the Earth element) provides the harshest unforgiving terrain and unrelenting topography to be conquered on the planet's surface, often aided by equally inclement shifts in weather. The planet is also home to many examples of extreme land-bound wildlife.

Figure 1: The Endless Challenge (© Shutterstock)

The following excerpt from American poet and writer Muriel Strode's poem Wind-Wafted *Wild Flowers* (1903) aptly describes such overall adventure: 'I will not follow where the path may lead, but I will go where there is no path, and I will leave a trail …'[1]

The less extreme alternative to personally challenging oneself in endurance activities can simply be attending celebratory festivals with unusual and sometimes quirky themes. This permits participants to dress in period costumes of historical significance or simply to make a statement, and have as much fun as possible. Participants may dress as clowns, wear various ritualistic masks or perhaps become covered in coloured powder while taking part in 'flour wars'. These worldwide festivals enable participants to briefly masquerade as somebody else and to enjoy such obscurity whilst conducting joyous mayhem and merriment – an extreme of life rarely encountered in daily life.

So why do so many people attempt to push themselves to the limit of their physical prowess and mental stamina? What is meant by being on the edge in the context of extreme life, such as personal competitive endurance pursuits? When you're 'on the edge', you're overcoming the physical limitations of the surrounding environment (Air, Water, Earth), and finding within yourself the essential motivation and 'spirit' to succeed.

The edge suggests some reasonably defined boundary that one reaches and then pulls back, for fear of failing or even perishing. It would seem that the personal rewards for succeeding in one's endeavours apparently far outweigh the potential for disaster. The major achievement would have to be building an unquestioning confidence in oneself to succeed (and to survive as well).

The downside of being 'on the edge' is that a person's body may be unable to withstand the rigors of endurance, and thus the adventurer fails to complete the challenge, or even fails to survive it.

I can only assume that many of those attempting to achieve the most extreme of feats produced by nature might agree with the following sentiment by naturalist and physicist Chet Raymo (1985):

> 'I am a child of the Milky Way. The night is my mother. I am made of the dust of stars. Every atom in my body was forged in a star ...'[2]
> Are we that indestructible?

For the animals, birds and marine life who may also live on the edge, it is more about survival than mere motivation to succeed.

FREE FALL

SKYDIVING

What motivates a human being to jump from a fixed wing light aircraft generally from 3 - 4.6 kilometres above the Earth's surface wearing little more than a tightly-fitted jump suit, safety helmet, goggles and a lightweight, compact parachute?

The obvious answer is to experience the overwhelming exhilaration of free falling through space, albeit for a few short minutes or less, until deploying the safety parachute.

The jumper may also be attempting to achieve the maximum possible vertical speed during the jump ('speed skydiving') by applying different falling positions or perhaps by wearing modified apparel. The aim may be to link together with other like-minded skydivers in formations of various complex configurations until the final moment before the parachute deploys.

Above all, the motivation is the personal adrenaline rush experienced while descending through the air unassisted and succumbing to the planet's gravity pull. Such precious time is relatively limited by any measure, given that light aircraft can only realistically fly at prescribed altitudes without additional regulatory approval. At higher altitudes, the need for a supplementary supply of oxygen is mandatory as the air becomes increasingly oxygen deficient.

FREE FALL

The time required to slow this descent sufficiently by deploying the parachute (to avoid a calamitous landing) leaves limited remaining time to free fall. This is quite a conundrum. To maximise this available time means skydiving from considerably higher altitudes.

The most recent record for the longest time spent in free fall has been achieved in October 2014 by a skydiver who was released from a helium-filled scientific balloon over New Mexico, USA, at an incredible 41.4 kilometres above sea level. He deployed his parachute at an altitude 5.5 km, thereby achieving the longest freefall distance and vertical speed in a time of 4 minutes and 27 seconds.[1] At such extreme altitudes, a special pressure suit was essential for survival.

For traditional skydivers, the optimum free fall time available is more like about one minute, and only nominally more from a maximum altitude of around 4.6 kilometres. It may seem very short, but I presume that when one is travelling at a constant speed of 193 kph – known as the 'terminal velocity' – time passes very quickly.

Terminal velocity occurs during a free fall when a person's falling body experiences zero acceleration and thus cannot go any faster. Their air speed remains stable (193 kph), caused by air resistance ('drag') which slows the body down.[2]

Speed skydivers experiment with different free fall techniques in order to reduce the effects of this 'drag' and thus travel at higher velocities. This usually involves a combination of scientific experimentation and lots of imaginative hope. By diving head first and keeping all limbs close to the body, or wearing a aerodynamically modified jump suit, higher speeds, perhaps exceeding 500 kph, seem achievable.[3] The speed achieved by the skydiver who left the helium balloon at an immense altitude was a staggering 1,323 kph. Now that really is free falling at its best.

PARACHUTE BASE JUMPING

Skydiving had its earliest origins in the 1930s, when parachutists began performing for the public. It eventually became officially accepted as an international sport by the World Air Sports Federation in 1951.[4] However, there are many variations and types of skydiving, so I will focus only on some extreme examples where many risk factors are in play for successful completion of the activity.

When one chooses to skydive from substantially lower altitudes than achieved in an aeroplane, B.A.S.E jumping appears amongst the most popular. This acronym distinguishes four separate fixed exit points from which one jumps: **B**uilding, **A**ntenna, **S**pan [bridge] and **E**arth [geological formations, such as a cliff]. I prefer to focus on skydiving from the Earth's naturally steep to vertical terrain, such as cliffs, escarpments and mountain sides.

WINGSUITING

When attempting BASE jumping, the skydiver may elect for a lightweight parachute to slow the descent, or opt for wingsuit flying plus a parachute. A wingsuit is made of modern flexible fabrics that add surface area to the skydiver's body, notably between the legs and under the arms. It then provides additional lift for the falling body, permitting the skydiver to effectively glide during the descent.

Various controlled movements of the skydiver's torso, shoulders, hips or knees alter the wingsuit's flight characteristics and subsequently the relative speed and direction of free fall. Unlike speed skydiving from an aircraft, wingsuiting attempts to drastically slow down the vertical free fall process and thereby increase the gliding distance towards a designated safe landing point. This is eventually assisted by the parachute deployment.

Figure 2: Wingsuiting (© Shutterstock)

This means a wingsuit flyer advances horizontally through the air, and can attain speeds up to 100 kph.[5]

Wingsuit flying is largely a modern phenomenon, progressing rapidly from the mid-1990s, with wingsuits being manufactured using technologically superior fabrics and various air flow design refinements.

Of the various wingsuit flight records achieved in this era, the longest duration of flight and the greatest horizontal distance flown are most notable. The longest flight was in Colombia in 2012 and lasted a remarkable nine minutes and six seconds,[6] whilst the greatest horizontal distance – an impressive 26.9 kilometres – was achieved in California in the same year.[7]

For the longest verified wingsuit BASE jump (from a mountain), a record of 7.5 kilometres was attained in Switzerland in 2011; it lasted a mere three minutes and twenty seconds of flight time.[8]

If '…speed skydiving is sometimes referred to as the fastest sport in the world without an engine'[9], then wingsuiting should simply be described as '…human body flight. Or body flying…'[10]

Wingsuiters can exit from an aircraft, thereby utilising the *relative* airflow generated by the forward speed of the aeroplane. However, in BASE jumping applications off mountains or from other airborne craft (such as hot air balloons), the vertical drop using gravity is required for the wingsuiter to generate enough air speed to gain sufficient lift. Both techniques can be hazardous and subject to the vagaries of prevailing weather at altitude and during descent.

Possibly what ultimately makes both BASE jumping and wingsuit flying extreme sports and substantially more life-endangering than skydiving, are the factors that may influence the free fall flight, particularly when jumping from various high fixed structures and achieving the maximum possible speed. The dangers include obstructions encountered at the exit point (cliffs, towers, tall buildings for example), obstructions during the jump/flight activity, and collisions with other participants.

BUNGEE JUMPING

Bungee/bungy jumping is amongst the most recent of extreme leisure activities of the modern era, and involves free-falling headfirst through the air with both feet tethered by an elasticised stretchable cord attached either to a high fixed structure or an aircraft hovering at a fixed height. It originated in ancient times as a land-diving ritualistic initiation for young men entering manhood on Pentecost Island in Vanuatu, and relied upon vines attached to their ankles absorbing the ground impact.[11]

It was revived in the late 1970s when three members of the *Oxford University Dangerous Sports Club* bungee-jumped from the 76m high Clifton Suspension Bridge in Bristol.[12] Within 3 years, they had jumped from many other bridges, as well as mobile cranes and hot air balloons.

FREE FALL

The adrenalin 'rush' of bungee jumping comes from the ability to free fall from a great height and partly rebound without injury. This is stringently dependent upon the correct length and quality of the elastic cord attached to one's feet to achieve a sufficiently safe recoil at the end of the fall. The cord expands until the bungee jumper reaches the end of the fall, then contracts/recoils sharply.

This leisure pursuit is not for the faint-hearted, medically restricted or otherwise of unfit health. Imagine plunging face-first toward the ground/river below after leaping off a high tower or other tall launching structure, only to rebound as the cord 'catches' you almost upon reaching the earth/river and being propelled upwards. There are also possible variations in performing the jump, including jumping backwards or hanging by hands or feet before releasing, just to add some further challenges.[13]

Some of the world's longest jumps from a fixed structure (dams, bridges, towers and topographical features) have ranged between 200 metres to 321 metres, but jump distances increase dramatically if leaping from a hot air balloon or helicopter. Due the difficulty in accurately quantifying distances between the moveable jump-site and the ground below, such measurements do not stand as official records.

However in 1989, one notable bungee jump performed by an early pioneer of the sport from a hot air balloon in California, was recorded as 670 metres. This height certainly added a few more precious invigorating seconds to the free fall.

UP AND AWAY

BALLOONING

The thought of flying away in a hot air balloon immediately conjures expectations of exhilaration and anticipation of the event, the tranquillity of floating high above the ground's surface, and the vista of majestic panoramic views stretching to the horizon. Contemporary poet Evrod Samuel succinctly captures these evocative sentiments in the 2015 poem *If Only I Could Fly* as follows in part:

> 'I wish I could grow some wings
> And soar up to the edge of the sky
> Where heaven touches the earth
> And the atmosphere protects
> All that dwell beneath
>
> I want to feel the delights of the wind
> Blowing in my face
> As I surf through the thin air

UP AND AWAY

Carefree and happy

I want to see what the avian [bird] world sees
As they effortlessly glide
Way up in the sky
Viewing both far and near

I want to cruise high above
Just as the jetliners do
Higher than a hot air balloon
That always seems so lonely
In the early morning sky …

… No one will be as high as me
I will be the king of the sky
Happy as a lark
Dancing among the clouds
And smiling at the sun …

… Up and up I will go
I will let the wind decide where I will flow.'[1]

For those electing adventurous and relatively graceful flight in such a craft, there are two different types of balloons: enclosed balloons filled with hydrogen or helium (though the gas to fill these is rather expensive), or the more common hot air balloons powered by artificially-heated air retained within the balloon's 'envelope'.

The latter is far more popular and uses the successful principle that the heated air is lighter than air surrounding the balloon, and thus causes the craft to become buoyant and to rise. Continuing to heat the air for a period using a flame burner enables the balloon to gain further altitude. Descending is achieved by either reduced rates of heating or selectively releasing the warm air from the balloon.

Flight durations are almost always confined to a single day, or typically

Figure 3: Ballooning (© Shutterstock)

to daylight hours in the case of helium balloons, which require the sun's warmth to prevent the helium gas from cooling and causing an unplanned descent.

Hot air ballooning has a vast array of challenges, particularly susceptibility to weather changes. As this craft can only change its direction of travel upwards or downwards, its horizontal movement over terrain is subject to the vagaries of wind. At higher altitudes, winds aloft can also be particularly unpredictable and fickle.

Inclement weather or unseasonal storms create unacceptable conditions for ballooning. Hot air balloons (those not using a combination of helium gas and hot air) must also remain within the earth's atmosphere to rely upon the effectiveness of heated air.

A balloon gradually wafts across the countryside on minimal air movement, and for the occupants standing or sitting inside the craft's attached gondola or wicker 'basket', the view can be spectacular and enduring.. The sturdy basket needs to be particularly strong, enough to carry the overall weight of up to fifteen people in some cases, as well as onboard supplies; and it must be robust/versatile enough to withstand repeated landings.[2]

It is not always the unpredicted change of weather that can impact dramatically on a balloon's flight and its landing, but collisions with other balloons in proximity or possibly land-based power lines.[3] The training and practical diligence of balloon pilots and their ground support crews remains critical to successful flights.

So what makes such an unusual form of aviation still remarkably popular, given its earliest origins of manned flight date back to the late 18th century? Perhaps the continuity of international balloon festivals held annually throughout the world may be a suitable indication.

The Albuquerque International Balloon Fiesta is a nine-day event convened in New Mexico, USA, and the largest such hot air balloon meeting in the world. In 2000, over 1,000 balloons were registered for the festival, but this has been trimmed in later years to a maximum permissible of 750.[4] However, the event is known for annually attracting more than 500 balloons.

The largest gathering in Europe is held over four consecutive days at the Bristol International Balloon Fiesta in England, and has grown to now exceed 100 registered balloons.[5]

The overriding attraction of hot air ballooning appears to be the immense pleasure gained from passengers obtaining a supreme aerial view of the world below. This form of leisure travel has fascinated humankind for centuries, and only in recent years appears to attracting many more participants. Some have succeeded in setting impressive world records.

In 1999, Bertrand Piccard and Brian Jones succeeded in being the first to traverse the world without landing their helium and hot air balloon. This covered a distance of 46,749 kilometres in almost 20 days.

In 2002, Steve Fossett was the first to complete the journey solo (after five previous attempts), in almost 15 days, also flying a helium and hot air balloon.[6] By 2016, this latter achievement was surpassed when Fedor Konyukhov completed the solo ballooning journey of 34, 820 kilometres in 11 days without landing.[7]

Why seek these impressive records against physically exhausting and almost insurmountable challenges flying through extreme and often precarious weather conditions at high altitude?

As Fedor Konyukhov noted during part of his world record journey over Antarctica whilst surviving on just four hours of sleep a day, '… This place feels very lonely and remote – no land, no planes, no ships'.[8] Why have people sought to be '…the first to challenge the realms of gods and winged creatures'?[9]

In some respects, it was the personal challenge of pushing ourselves beyond our perceived limits and barriers. Importantly, it was probably also the wonder and astonishment that mankind could actually lift '… off from the earth to soar in regions heretofore reserved for the celestial [the dominion of God or the gods]'.[10] An appropriate parallel would be the successful landing on the moon and a human being's first steps on an alien soil.

HANG GLIDING

For a rather different personal experience of free flight to higher altitudes, hang gliding offers the distinctive similarity of 'almost flying like a bird'. You are 'at one with nature's elements'. Hang gliding is not to be confused with paragliding, which usually tends to be of lower altitude, shorter duration (completed in less than an hour), and requires a discernibly different occupant position. Both rely upon the prevailing winds and upward air movements for their flights.

Most modern hang gliders comprise a rigid, lightweight alloy metal frame covered with synthetic sailcloth in the shape of a wing. The flier is suspended horizontally in a harness below this wing on an airframe, and uses body movements (such as shifting weight) to control flight.

Conversely, paragliders use a relatively flexible wing and fly in a more relaxed sitting position. However, hang gliders travel at considerably higher speeds – at least three times faster – and cover substantially greater distances. Hang gliding flights can last for hours – hang gliders can remain aloft longer due their design and equipment construction.[11]

The world record for straight distance by a hang glider was achieved on 4 July 2012, across Texas, USA, and covered 764 kilometres.[12] Diligent planning ensured the record attempt took place on the longest day of summer, and strong prevailing winds at that time were selected to provide the ideal weather conditions for continuous hang gliding.

The non-stop journey involved two hang gliders simultaneously attempting to exceed the same long-distance record, following relatively similar routes. It reportedly lasted almost 11 hours, optimising any regional 'thermals' or columns of rising hot air to prolong the elevation of both hang gliders until nightfall. As a glider in flight is continuously descending, rising air currents are needed to extend such flight. The new record holder Dustin B. Martin was eventually able to glide 5 kilometres further than his colleague by soaring on the very last thermal of daylight at the end of this considerable journey.[13]

The unlucky second flier (Jonny Durand) eventually returned to the same starting location in June 2016 in a concerted attempt to claim this world long-distance hang gliding record. His seven attempts were thwarted by a lack of suitably perfect 'thermals' to extend his flight, and the record would not be achieved.

Only a handful of hang glider pilots are willing to push past 480 km [to the world record of 764 km], as illustrated by Jonny Durand:

> 'Not everyone wants to be in the air for 11 hours and put themselves through that kind of pain. It's a mentally exhausting day, and physically exhausting obviously. It's the things we do for world records…
>
> …That's the day I'm looking for. I don't want to beat it [world long-distance record] by a mile, I want to beat it by 80 km'.[14]

Hang gliding usually requires fliers launch from high altitude areas to optimise their flight time in the air. For beginners, this would be from a hill or cliff, progressing to substantially higher features such as mountains, canyons or even from hot air balloons. The current world altitude record for a balloon-launched hang glider was established by Judy Leden in Jordan in 1994, and stands at 11,856 metres.[15]

'The ascent took 1 hour to complete and the descent 1.5 hours… despite experiencing a temperature of -62°C at 12,497 metres which caused slight frost bite to her face.'[16] Subsequently, 'In October 2002, Judy became Leonardo da Vinci's test pilot when she flew a glider, built from his 500 year old drawings. It was made using materials only da Vinci would have had access to…held together with leather straps and hemp string'.[17]

As with so many flying activities subject to prevailing weather, hang gliding is very dependent upon the experience, skill, stamina and training of the flier, who must rely heavily upon his or her safety harness and the structural integrity of the glider to avoid a potentially catastrophic outcome.

'In extreme hang gliding, experienced pilots perform full barrel rolls, inverted manoeuvres, and other stunt flying moves.'[18]

However, it is the following sentiment that most effectively captures the essence of hang gliding through the air:

> 'You can get so high that you can see the curvature of the Earth. You can soar with hawks and eagles off your wing tips. You can dive and swoop in the sky on a good day. You can drive like a race car in the sky.'[19]

BALL PIT DIVING

For those adults seeking a far less strenuous pastime than gliding through the atmosphere at high altitude, perhaps diving through the air into a massive 'ball pit' filled to capacity with thousands of small, hollow and multi-coloured plastic balls between 5.5 mm – 7.6 mm in diameter may be more suitable.

The 'ball pit' can be either a gigantic modified pool or a smaller, more compact box structure lined with non-allergic padding to cushion the effect of 'ball crawling' through the mass and to assist in any soft landing in the pit.

Even lying on such an enormous ocean of hollow spheres and pushing oneself along can be arduous, as these buoyant balls do not behave exactly like water. It depends upon what manoeuvres are being attempted across or under the balls.

Figure 4: The Ball Pit Beckons (© Shutterstock)

The non-toxic plastic balls can move *en masse* or individually, and given there may be between 50,000 and 1,000,000 crammed into an adult ball pit, it presents many variations to what may happen. In 2013, a hotel in Shanghai, China constructed a ball pit 12.6 m x 25 m, filled it with a million small plastic spheres and established a new Guinness World Record.[20]

By 2015, this record had been exceeded, again in China, with a massive 2,080,000 plastic balls filling the world's largest ball bath of 1,442.2 square metres.[21]

By any stretch of the imagination, this would certainly provide enough of a challenge for the most ardent ball pit diver. A variation on this achievement is a smaller ball pit of 1.1 million translucent plastic balls, which opened in January 2017 in Sydney, Australia. The translucent balls produce an unusual 'clear ocean effect' for those electing to dive into the pit and 'swim' the sea.[22]

AIR AND WATER

CLIFF DIVING

Ever get that feeling that it is going to be one of those days when everything goes wrong? A day when you might as well try some dramatic pastime, such as cliff diving.

There is quite a subtle difference between cliff diving and jumping off a cliff. Cliff diving requires head-first entry into the water below, preceded by a carefully executed and streamlined dive with rotation through the air. Conversely, cliff jumping usually means entering the water feet-first, pointing the body like a pencil with both arms positioned at the side and feet together to optimise entry. However, both feats may occur from same height of steep overhanging cliff and neither rely upon any special clothing or equipment.

It requires basic athletic prowess, coupled with an ample proportion of raw courage, determination and mental stamina, to face the considerable plunge into the natural stretch of water (ocean, lake, pond) far below.

ON THE EDGE

Figure 5: Cliff Diving (© Shutterstock)

So what makes cliff diving so special and extreme? In its simplest terms: 'The beautiful locations, the thrill of heights, the terrifying speeds …'[1]

Cliff diving is probably amongst the most precarious of extreme competitive sports. To appreciate the hazards of such a venture, it is important to think about the distances being dived/jumped, the state of the ocean below (waves, swell, nearby rocky outcrops, water clarity), and how the diver/jumper enters the water (awkward landing or smooth entry).

Assuming ideal conditions of the ocean and a near-perfect entry into the water, the height of the dive/jump remains a major factor. The higher the jump, the faster and more dangerous it becomes to hit the water. The most recent world record achieved for the highest cliff jump feet-first into a pool of water was in August 2015 in Switzerland, from a height of 58.8 metres.[2]

There are also additional factors to consider, including ensuring that you actually reach the water safely and not collide with the cliff or outcropping rocks on the descent, and once penetrating the water's surface, that it is

AIR AND WATER

sufficiently deep enough to preclude you striking the water body's floor. The depth of water can be as shallow as two metres or as deep as five metres, depending upon the waves. Deeper water is safer for the diver, and of course, the timing of the dive is critical.

Competitive cliff divers usually dive from heights of 18-27 metres, although the World High Diving Federation recommends that no one dives from 20 metres or higher [without at least two professional rescue scuba divers in the water] due to the high potential for injury.[3]

However, there are professional seasoned show cliff divers such as *The La Quebrada Cliff Divers* in Acapulco, Mexico, who routinely jump from 30 metres or 41 metres off the La Quebrada cliffs.

These divers are very familiar with the risks of diving into shallow water, having performed in the area for many years. They crucially time their dives according to fluctuating wave and water conditions. The 2002 Guinness Book of World Records lists this diving as the 'highest regularly performed headfirst dives' in the world.[4]

The tradition of cliff diving can be traced as far back as the 1920s, when an even greater height – 45 metres – was used.

To clearly appreciate the earliest recorded history of cliff diving/jumping, one needs to look to the Hawaiian island of Maui about 250 years ago.

A legendary warrior chief/king, aptly named after The God of Thunder, was the island's last independent ruler, and he demanded a rigorous and daunting test be performed to confirm the allegiance and mettle of his followers. They were forced to follow him in jumping feet-first from a high 63 foot (19 m) cliff [a hallowed ledge] into a shallow depth of ocean below. For those able to survive such an audacious act, their courage and tenacity would be proven beyond doubt.[5]

The legend also suggests that this king jumped/seemingly 'flew' from cliffs sometimes as high as around 120 metres just to display his supreme athletic prowess.[6] For his high flying jumps, he earned the nickname of 'Birdman' [The Birdman of Maui] from visiting English sailors. The Birdman also inspired the famous Hawaiian words "lela kawa", translated as 'jumping off high cliffs and entering the water feet-first without a splash'.[7]

Over time, this radical form of cliff 'jumping' was eventually performed either for an individual's personal challenge or more often to entertain tourists and the locals. It then evolved as recently as 2009 into a competitive diving sport, with the advent of the world's largest cliff diving competition known as the Red Bull Cliff Diving World Series. This would eventually span 23 countries across four continents.

Competitive cliff diving became based around a person's dive skills and distinctive style of diving, with the aim to minimise any water disturbance when breaking the ocean's surface. This may involve diving in many spectacular locations, such as Hawaii, Japan, Mexico, Greece, Brazil, Chile, and on the Azores Islands in the middle of the Atlantic Ocean, to name just a few places.[8]

'Tombstoning' is an interesting term sometimes used to describe the practice of cliff 'jumping' from a very high place. It may originate from a number of sources, particularly given the subtle connotation of extremely dangerous and potentially fatal outcomes resulting from such activity.[9] It may also have arisen from the straight vertical posture of a jumper's body as they enter the natural stretch of water, thus resembling a tombstone.[10]

Another possible explanation for the term may relate to a playful craze of people jumping from *Tombstone Rock* on the south coast of Devon in Britain in 1955, as then reported by the *Plymouth Herald*.[11] Regardless of its origins, the term 'tombstoning' clearly indicates possible dire consequences for this human leisure activity.

KITEBOARDING

Kiteboarding is yet another extreme leisure activity combining air (the power of the wind for propulsion) and water (the ocean's surface and waves). Participants travel on a *kiteboard* [small surfboard modified with/ without footstraps or thin rectangular wakeboard].

The kiteboarder harnesses the wind through a large controllable power/ traction kite of either aerofoil shape or with inflatable ribs and leading edge to retain its shape for relaunching when wet.

Figure 6: Kiteboarding (© Shutterstock)

In many respects, kiteboarding has combined various elements of other air/ water sports, including paragliding, windsurfing/sailboarding (a surfboard with attached sail), snowboarding and even skateboarding.

However, this extreme activity has some distinguishing features and a number of variations. These include kitesurfing of waves on a standard surfboard, wave jumping utilising the wind, speed kiteboarding, and long distance journeys across oceans and between countries.

> 'The history of kiteboarding is short, yet its growth has been staggering – it is by far the youngest water sport to enjoy the kind of participation numbers that it does, and is currently one

ON THE EDGE

of the fastest-growing sports on the planet.'[12]

There are several constraints to be overcome to successfully undertake kiteboarding, not the least being the physical strain the kiteboarder must withstand in order to steer the kite and control speed.

Negotiating waves, 'jumping' the kiteboard without the need for a launch wave, or travelling longer distances also require an appropriate standard of stamina. For those completely at home on kiteboards and readily capable of handling complex techniques or conditions, world records are readily achievable.

Figure 7: Kite Surfer Jumping over Water during Surfing in Red Sea, Eilat, Israel. Editorial credit: Rostislav Glinsky/Shutterstock.com

In terms of kiteboarder speed records, the current world record speed of 107.4 kph was achieved in November 2017 by French rider Alex Caizergues at Salin de Giraud on the Compagnie des Salins waterway in France.[13]

The highest kite jump world record of 28.6 metres, with an airtime of 8.5 seconds, was set in February 2017 by Nick Jacobsen in Cape Town, South

Africa during 40 knot (74 kph) winds.[14]

However, long distance kiteboarder records certainly provide quite an insight into the prowess of these individuals. Louis Tapper completed the longest recorded kite journey/solo passage, undertaking an incredible 2000 kilometre kitesurf between Salvador and Sao Luis, Brazil. The journey took 30 days, between July/August 2010. Incredibly, Tapper used only one kiteboard and didn't have a support crew.[15]

In the 21st century, the popularity of long distance kiteboarding races has meant a 40 kilometre event between islands in the Baltic Sea attracted 400 contestants. Similar numbers are drawn to the world-class Lancelin Ocean Classic off the rugged, scenic and wind-swept Western Australian coastline.

Kiteboarding has its roots in the motivation of some people to experiment at various times with man-lifting kites as an alternative mode of travel over water. This was to accelerate in the latter part of the 20th century with the development of superior kite fabrics combined with various leisure transport such as surfboards, canoes, buggies and a range of skis for example.

Kiteboarding really came of age in the 1990s. Improved kite designs and the manufacture of specialised kiteboards resulted in an immense increase in popularity worldwide amongst those seeking such extreme sports. Kiteboarding is now recognised as a mainstream sport and continues to generate innovative design and technique developments.

However, unlike many other popular water sports, the development of modern kiteboarding occurred almost simultaneously in a number of different directions. One of these directions is 'wakestyle kiteboarding', and not to be confused with 'wakeboarding' (where a short rectangular board is towed behind a water-ski boat).

Wakestyle kiteboarding involves the rider wearing '…wakeboarding "boots" for their kiteboard (as opposed to straps and pads), ensuring their feet remain firmly attached at all times … This style is also associated with performing [difficult] powered [aerial] tricks with the kite as low to the water as possible …'[16]

EXTREME WATER PURSUITS

SURFING

What do the following bay and harbour locations: Banzai Pipeline, Waimea Bay, Oahu (Hawaii); Jaws (Pe'ahi) (Hawaii); Maui (Hawaii); Outer Bombie/The Right, Cowaramup Bay (Western Australia); and Mavericks, Pillar Point Harbour (Northern California) have in common?

Given the right weather and ocean conditions at various times of the year, and the surrounding physiography and hydrography of these locales, monstrous surf breaks can be produced. These bays and harbours have the world's biggest waves. These are gigantic waves that may crest out at least 15-20 metres, and occasionally at 24 metres, or even an estimated 30 metres from trough to crest (such a wave was recorded off the coast of Nazaré in Portugal[1,2]).

To fully appreciate the scale of these waves, we can compare them to buildings. They are as tall as two to four storey office buildings.[3] All the surfers have between these daunting waves and their bodies is a sleek fibreglass surfboard, their surfing expertise and a considerable dose of courage to conquer the oncoming behemoth.

'Big waves are not measured in feet [metres] and inches [centimetres], but in increments of fear.'[4]

Of course, there are other various wave characteristics to be considered for extreme board surfing, depending upon what the surfer is seeking.

One particularly important facet is the 'heaviness' of a wave, which is '… the volume of water pouring over in the lip of the curl, as opposed to the shallowness of the reef the water is pouring over …', and there are many heavy surf spots worldwide, including Jaws in Maui and Mavericks in USA.[5]

However, it is Teahupoo ('Chopes') in Tahiti which is thought to be the megabeast of such heavy surf breaks. It forms when massive incoming open-ocean swells encounter a shallow barrier reef atop a deep underwater cliff in the middle of the South Pacific, with dramatic consequences. Surfers have learned that in order to survive such a prolific and intimidating meat-grinder total respect is required.

Extreme surfing is associated with a considerable degree of personal risk. Serious injuries may arise from the severe forces of the breaking waves, perhaps through becoming enveloped by the wave, or through being thrown against underlying sharp coral reefs or abrasive rocky outcrops. There is also drowning of course.

The personal challenges can be enormous, but there is always yet another wave waiting to be surfed somewhere, preferably offering the longest unhindered ride of all.

BODYBOARDING

Another group of surfers who are routinely exposed to many of these hazards are bodyboarders. This group rely upon lying, kneeling/crouching or sometimes standing on short, rectangular-shaped 'boogie boards' manufactured of a hydrodynamic foam; they use portable swim fin(s) on hands and feet to control the board's movement and direction.

The versatility offered by such bodyboards has enabled participants in this extreme sport to successfully accomplish many complex and challenging aerial manoeuvres on a diverse range of waves.

The Hawaiian bodyboarder Mike Stewart was one of the pioneers of this sport. This nine-time World Champion and accomplished big wave surfer has shown us that great waves can be conquered even riding the smallest of surfboards.

WHITEWATER KAYAKING

For an equivalent inland extreme pursuit, whitewater kayaking would have to be as challenging, particularly as a kayak is not just a canoe. Kayakers sit inside the vessel and use a double-bladed paddle to propel and guide the vessel. Canoeists typically kneel or half-kneel and use a paddle with only one blade.

The kayak sits low-to-the-water with a closed deck to preclude flooding if capsized, or a flexible water proof 'sprayskirt' to prevent water entering, and a cockpit where the paddler sits. Inflatable rubber rafts can also be popular for this type of wild kayaking.[6]

The design shape, size and length of kayaks varies immensely. Specialised kayaks for negotiating whitewater rapids and extremely turbulent waterways need to be tough and durable, yet easily manoeuvrable. They must offer adequate stability and buoyancy to survive severe buffeting by whitewater or encounters with rocky outcrops/submerged hazards, and must readily resurface if 'rolled' by the kayaker.

Kayaks are moulded in semi-rigid, high impact plastic to remain structurally sound. With model names like *Flying Squirrel* and *Stomper*, these kayaks are destined for rugged passage.

For kayakers seeking the ultimate personal exhilaration, 'creeking' (kayaking on streams and rivers with rapids) is the perfect choice. Creeking could be described as '…likely to include…running ledges, slides, and waterfalls on relatively small and tight rivers [of high gradient] …', though does not necessarily exclude some very large and big volume rivers.[7]

It is the introduction of excessively turbulent, high volume water and a considerable number of outcropping rocks in a confined river bed that substantially increases the speed the kayaker must employ to successfully traverse these obstacles.

Figure 8: Whitewater Kayaking (© Shutterstock)

ON THE EDGE

The Norwegian Fjords

Probably the best way to comprehend this extreme pursuit is to examine some of the world's many challenging whitewater venues and what makes them so exciting to kayakers. The fjords of western Norway, arguably amongst the steepest and wildest rivers on the planet, have to rate highly on this scale.

These fjords have a series of cascading waterfalls interspersed between innumerable rock ledges and bedrock mini-drops, and this means kayakers are not permitted much recovery time before reaching the next set of waterfalls or further rapids lurking along the route.[8]

One of the most difficult manoeuvres for a whitewater kayaker is 'running'

Figure 9: Yet Another Waterfall (© Shutterstock)

waterfalls along the river's route. There are realistically only two options for such a risky endeavour, and both involve choosing the right angle of entry into the landing area below. Both are strictly guidelines and require careful consideration before attempting.

For non-vertical or relatively low drop waterfalls with landing zones of shallow depth, the kayak should land flat, hopefully assisted by an abundant cushion of highly aerated water in this zone. Extreme caution is still required nonetheless.

For steeper, high waterfalls with substantial deep water at the base, the entry could be approached more vertically by 'pencilling' into the water. It is also crucial to first confirm the depth of water for a safe landing beforehand. 'The more aerated the water is, the less vertical you need to be as the landing will be more cushioned.'[9] The kayakers still always need to protect themselves when hitting the water below during such manoeuvres.

A rather peculiar phenomenon that may be found below a waterfall, as well as in constricted rapids or canyons, and randomly on large rivers, resembles '…bubbles in a pot of boiling water'. This unpredictable surge of aerated water occurs when it '…is finding its way back up to the surface after having plummeted toward the bottom'.[10] Wild water going up and down right where you are landing heralds quite a time for a kayaker!

Yarlung-Tsangpo River

Extreme kayaking conditions can also be found in mountainous Tibet along the Yarlung-Tsangpo River. Like Norway in one respect, the water is icy and treacherous, originating from the freezing mountain peaks of the region. However, it also dissects the highest parts of the Himalayas through towering gorges, and consequently may become a raging torrent of muddy water at times.

'The Tsangpo Gorge cuts through the eastern end of the Himalayas to form the deepest, most remote river canyon on earth. Three times deeper than the Grand Canyon, hemmed in by 7500 metre plus peaks,…'[11]

Traversing such an unforgiving, high gradient and massive river with its contrasting extremes of rapids, fast-flowing waters and confined ravine faces can be particularly daunting for many kayakers. Once beset with mountain flood waters, the tortuous route becomes virtually unpassable, or at least carries a high risk of potentially catastrophic consequences for travellers.

The river's name in the Tibetan language translates as 'water comes from snowy mountains' and this water is prolific. The Yarlung-Tsangpo River is the country's longest waterway, with a length of 2,057 kilometres across Tibet, and an overall length of 2,840 kilometres taken across neighbouring countries.[12]

Too much fast flowing water and unexplored terrain can be quite sobering even for the most proficient kayaker.

The Rio Santo Domingo River

There have been some extraordinary records set by extreme whitewater kayakers. In 2013, three hearty adventurers jointly traversed the steepest navigable stretch of the notorious Rio Santo Domingo River in Central America in a previously unattained single descent.

This remarkable river stretches through the mountains of Guatemala and southern Mexico and has a consecutive series of very closely spaced waterfalls with little intervening space, much like a set of stairs. A kayaker misjudging these manoeuvres would be flushed down the remaining waterfalls as if a sluice gate was opening.

The Apurímac River

One of the most highly rated whitewater sources in South America is the Apurímac River in south-western Peru that (before joining other rivers) traverses 700 kilometres of deep and narrow mountainous gorges and canyons, interrupted by falls and rapids in various sections.[13]

These are not the world's largest or most spectacular whitewater rapids, but can be particularly treacherous for small craft like kayaks that may be enveloped by the sheer turbulence, rock undercuts and variety of rapids. The river's descent from the mountain ridges is fed by icy snowmelt waters and its translated name of 'Speaker of the Gods' or 'The God Talker' (native Quechua language) heralds quite a challenge ahead for intrepid kayakers.

RIVER FLOAT RAFTING

By comparison to whitewater kayaking, river float rafting would appear rather subdued. Floating serenely along in the current of a gently flowing river firmly lodged in an inflated heavy duty truck inner tube would definitely be considered anything but extreme. Even with three floats linked together for group rafting, the passage remains placid.

Such industrial float tubes are usually repurposed for aquatic recreational use, and if one decided to tackle river conditions with a few more physical challenges, they would need to be resilient and durable.

Take for example a wide river with reasonably fast flowing water, small riffles and strong swirling eddies, but only occasional submerged obstructions; or perhaps a narrower dipping channel of shallow cascading water created by erosion of a massive bedrock. This is when the river float bounces and bobs along at quite a frenetic pace. Hold on tightly because this may become quite a tortuous ride.

For those kayakers pursuing even more aquatic challenges, squirt boats might just provide them. These very small, ultra-low-volume kayaks are designed to work with the currents below the water's surface, and are thus customised for a tight almost uncomfortable fit around the kayaker.

They permit the rider to manoeuvre in eddy lines or pourovers in a river while virtually submerged for as long as possible, thereby optimising even minor available currents. Squirt boats provide a totally new and rather extreme approach to kayaking by staying low in the water or underwater to fully utilise the available whitewater. They can become connected with the water.[14]

ON THE EDGE

Figure 10: Not That Easy (© Shutterstock)

FREEDIVING

Freediving is an unforgiving recreational activity relying upon descending below the water holding one's breath as long as practicable until resurfacing. The freediver does not rely upon any breathing equipment.

Freedivers may utilise diving apparatus such as a face mask, or dive enhancing equipment such as bifins/monofin and a suitably weighted object to expedite their descent, and when returning to the surface; use inflatable vests or bags, or pull themselves upwards along a sturdy 'safety' line.

The riskiest freediving attempts are those where the divers strive to descend increasingly deeper than most humans can tolerate and to stay longer at those depths.

The present men's world record holder for No-Limits Apnea ('temporary cessation of breathing') in open water, as recognised by one of the world's two associations for competitive freediving, achieved a depth of 214 metres in 2007.[15] This classification permits the diver to use any means of breath-holding dive to reach final depth and return to surface.

What is most interesting about this depth is that it is almost on the limit that any human body can freedive and survive. American journalist and author James Nestor provides some informative elaboration on such topics:

> 'At sixty feet [18 metres] down,… most humans can make it to this depth and feel the changes [heart beat slows by half, lungs shrink, senses numb] … At three hundred feet [91 metres], we are profoundly changed. The pressure at these depths is ten times that of surface [heart beat slows to quarter rate, senses disappear, brain enters a dream state]…At six hundred feet [183 metres] down, …the ocean's pressure–twenty times that of surface–is too extreme for most human bodies to withstand… At eight hundred feet [244 metres] down appears to be an absolute limit, … risk paralysis and death to go beyond that depth.'[16]

So what entices some of us to freedive to such extreme ocean depths and thus be exposed to a myriad of aquatic hazards, including intense cold seawater temperatures, increasing underwater pressure and temporary loss of crucial life functions?

The risk to human life can be enormous, from loss of consciousness and serious organ damage to drowning. Acclaimed US author James Nestor boldly exclaims 'Other than BASE jumping… freediving is the most dangerous adventure sport in the world…It feels like a death wish'.[17]

What motivates freedivers who continue to push the boundaries and physical limitations of the human body with increasingly deeper dives?

It is probably the same motivation that entices people to freedive through underwater caves and cavern systems – namely the exhilaration of exploration on a limited air supply. However, with cave diving the risks also increase profoundly because of underwater currents, obstructions, limited visibility and navigational disorientation.

Figure 11: Exhaled Air Bubbles of the Freediver (© Shutterstock)

SNOW AND ICE

POLAR SWIMMING

Liquid freshwater freezes naturally to solid ice at 0° Celsius in colder climes (or minus 2° Celsius for saltwater), but this does not preclude a select few from still enjoying the frigid temperatures or the extreme inconvenience of submerging in the shivering water located beneath the surface ice.

Some may liken this outdoor pursuit to that of polar bears who frequent the Arctic regions. Over most of the world, there are avid groups of swimmers of all ages who belong to the *Polar Bear Club*, or similarly named winter bathing clubs. In warmer countries, these groups are active only in the cool winter months, when the seawater does not freeze over but plunges in temperature. In the colder frozen regions of the planet, swimming in extremely cold water occurs throughout the year.

To plunge into either sub-zero salty seawater or freezing freshwater, albeit briefly, both require considerable stamina and keen determination. A contributory factor in one's decision to take part in non-competitive ice swim-

ON THE EDGE

Figure 12: Chilled Out (© Shutterstock)

ming could be that the ambient temperature above the water may be colder than in the water, with the chilling effect of any breeze or wind adding a further chill factor.

TOUR SKATING

Many of us would be aware of cross-country snow trekking/skiing where skiers use narrow lightweight skis for optimum traction when travelling across undisturbed or tracked snow, or even snow shoes where hiking is preferred through steeper countryside. The innumerable and often precarious hazards encountered when traversing snow-bound terrain can be onerous.

Now consider an alternative – perhaps you are required to skate for long distances across considerable ice tracts of frozen streams, lakes and sea. Where such travel crosses open ice on the sea or covering lakes, this is called *Nordic ice skating*, and is a popular form of touring or 'wild skating' in Scandinavian countries.

Where skaters follow marked routes along canals or lakes, such as in the Netherlands, it is known as *Dutch (toer) skating*. Both types of skating are conducted for leisure purposes rather than purely for travelling.[1]

Figure 13: Let's Get Started (© Shutterstock)

Skating over frozen rivers, lakes and sometimes across the sea has a considerable pioneering history as a common means of travel in various countries, especially in the Netherlands, where it has been practiced for several centuries:

> 'Communication between important centres of commerce is maintained chiefly by canals, and when they become closed to navigation by ice, the frozen surface afforded a ready and rapid means of locomotion. Dutch men and women habitually made use of these ice highways; young Dutchwomen have been known to skate to market, carrying their infants and their basket of eggs.'[2]

However, it is long distance 'tour' skating on open ice across large bodies of water that appears to me to present the most diverse challenges.

Canada in the late 19th century, for example, was still largely reliant upon rivers for lumber and fishing, and consequently travel along extensive frozen rivers required a very special type of skate. The 'Long Reach Speed Skate' with a blade 45 centimetres in length was designed around 1870 to fulfil this purpose. This unique invention (known as a Long Reacher) permitted '…an able-bodied young man to skate this distance [about 129 kilometres] in little under seven hours'.[3]

Such long blades permitted the skater to glide more easily, with less digging into ice than happens with conventional skates, and thus they are suited to the uneven and soft ice which may be encountered when travelling across large bodies of frozen water. Endurance rather than speed is the common factor.

Most long distance skating tours in the modern era appear to be conducted over frozen lakes and along the larger rivers. They all share one common skating hazard – ice. However, there are several different types of ice formed in nature, dependent upon factors such as prevailing climatic conditions, presence/absence of snow, excessive rain, seawater, and the degree of thawing/melting of the various ice layers.

Ice formed over seawater can be weakened and softened by the salt crystals present, whilst snow falling into freezing water can form ice that is '… generally rougher, softer and weaker than black ice', and snow falling onto ice may cause it to soak up the additional moisture ('soak ice'). The ideal for distance skaters is the very first ice to form in suitably good weather ('black ice'), as it is smooth, clean, strong and relatively continuous.[4]

Skaters may have to endure numerous other ice-related hazards while skating for many kilometres across wild regions. These include the consistency of ice (uniformity of thickness and quality) encountered, the extent and depth of evident cracking and thawing, and the presence of hidden hazards, such as visually deceptive soft snow drifts or protruding frozen vegetation.

A skater's poor judgement in avoiding the potentially disastrous weaker, softer and thin ice areas may result in falling through the ice layer or tripping face-first in sharp, unforgiving ice shards. Simply staying on your feet may not an easy feat!

Tour skating, trip skating or simply 'wild skating' over significant bodies of frozen water such as the sea has to be amongst one of the most extreme personal events that can experienced, as subtly illustrated by the pioneering Finnish poet and writer Otto Manninen in part of *Skating on the Sea*:

> 'Unfrozen the dim inner waters below,
> but hidden in solid ice below:
> of the foaming billows underneath
> there is neither sound nor trace.
>
> Unfrozen, the depths are rushing below,
> but on top is a level bridge:
> whee! they can slip and slide about,
> leaving no groove or ridge.
>
> Above, play is wild and laughter is loud,
> steel shoes all brightness and youth:
> over the ice they merrily race,
> the lid on the gulfs is smooth…
>
> …It leads them to stretches blue with dusk
> where is no more buoy or mark:
> no thought of black night surprising, no cure
> about coming home in the dark,
>
> nor any sense, already amid
> unknown expanses of sea,
> of night descending to weave all round
> a moonlit mystery,
>
> of having plumbed the inner depths
> to the point of drowning, where joy
> with its capering burden already feels

the floor giving way, ...'[5]

SNOWBOARDING

Snowboarding is a leisure activity particularly suitable to descending snow-covered alpine slopes. It has similar fundamental elements to several other recreational pursuits, including skiing, tobogganing, skateboarding and surfing, as well as many sports that rely upon correct body balance and positioning ('stance'), such as golf, cricket or bowling.

In simplest terms, the snowboarder rides in an upright position with both feet attached by bindings to a single flat 'snowboard' that is wider than conventional skis.

The historical design and purpose of snowboards closely reflects that of surfboard development, in that snowboarders ride '...deep powder (soft snow) – which most closely resembles the feeling of surfing – rather than on hard pack and icy slopes'.[6]

Although snowboard design, materials and construction continue to evolve, the main commercial types are used for the most common styles of riding.

These include extreme and spontaneous versatility on natural, un-groomed terrain (free-ride); freestyle (snowboarding with performing tricks); free-carving on hard packed snow or groomed runs (similar to turning a surfboard through waves); or fast racing on wide open terrain with room to move.[7]

The most important skill to snowboarding is possibly the freedom to express oneself in various combinations of riding techniques without coming to grief, including launching into the air off ramps or slopes ('getting air'), or mastering a myriad of intricate airborne or skiing manoeuvres.

SNOW AND ICE

Figure 14: Riding Powder Snow - I am Flying (© Shutterstock)

The challenge lays in overcoming the extreme range of difficult hazards that may exist on steep snow slopes or in untouched fresh snowdrifts. The injury rate for snowboarding is around double that of alpine skiing, although beginners with insufficient snowboarding experience or training probably account for most of these injuries.[8] While experienced riders are less likely to suffer injury, the injuries they do sustain tend to be more severe.[9]

Apart from the obvious falls possible whilst undertaking tricky manoeuvres on snow slopes, collisions with others at speed may account for many injuries. However, snowboarding on unprepared runs or across unfamiliar/unmarked terrains present far more risk, due to such hazards as buried rocks, ice crevasses and potential local snow avalanches.

Snowboarding is not like many other similar individual ice/snow-based sports where world records are routinely achieved, as it has mostly developed for leisure purposes. It has gradually evolved into a recognised Olym-

ON THE EDGE

pic sport, but retains its origins of performing merely for the enjoyment, albeit extreme enjoyment at times.

Two acknowledged world records worth noting involve unusual accomplishments.

The current world speed snowboarding record was set in April 2015 by Frenchman Edmond Plawczyk, wearing hard-shell boots. Edmond set an incredible pace of 203 kph on a slope considered to be the fastest in the world: 1,400 metres in length with a 435 metre vertical descent.[10] It was not as fast as a speed skiing record, but was certainly impressive for snowboarding.

The other world record was achieved in 2007 when Norwegian Terje Håkosen set the 'highest air' jump, rising 9.8 m whilst performing a backside 360o spin and still landing correctly.[11] 'Getting air' in snowboarding provides the rider with the immeasurable feeling of floating free and weightless through the air, if only for a few precious moments.

Both records provided these proficient snowboarders with the desired outcome – enjoying this exhilarating pastime to the maximum.

Not a bad outcome for a device contrived in the modern era as a sled: the first snowboard was actually two children's skis fastened together so as to permit a child to stand on 'the resultant board/plank' whilst gliding down a snow slope.[12]

THE SURGING AQUA

WATERSPOUTS

Waterspouts are a particularly frightening phenomena for seafaring folk. They are usually a non-supercell tornado passing over the sea or large lakes and are most commonly found in the tropics and subtropical areas, including the Indian and Pacific Oceans, as well as seasonally in temperate areas such as in the Atlantic Ocean and Baltic regions.

They may form in thunderstorm clouds or other cumulus-type clouds, often originating in groups from one parent cloud. However, waterspouts share one acoustic similarity– terrifying roars, howls and hissing sounds.[1] Their features include forming without much warning, moving at modest speeds before decaying after a short-lived duration (generally 15-20 minutes), and extremes of wind strength.[2]

As they do not take-up any dust or debris passing over water, the columnar vortex remains partly and sometimes entirely invisible to the eye. At the end of development of the vortex ('funnel'), the waterspout takes on a very long and curved rope-like form. They destroy or break-up small boats.[3] However, many waterspouts, despite their rather ominous spiralling vortices, are non-destructive as long as they remain over water and develop during fair weather conditions.

Figure 15: Waterspout at Sea (© Shutterstock)

The largest outbreak of waterspouts recorded in history was over the Great Lakes on the border between Canada and the US, and lasted for seven days in the autumn of 2003. In total, an unbelievable 66+ waterspouts [freshwater] were sighted in this period![4]

Various historical records of maritime damage and destruction – encompassing the 18th -19th centuries, and into the 20th century – have noted sailing vessels and steamboats being de-masted, capsized or sunk by such ocean whirlwinds (sometimes seen in 'swarms'). Many ships record only incurring minor damage, but none recommended sailing through such waterspouts.[5]

If the following eyewitness account of a waterspout in 1954 is suitably accurate, that advice is certainly wise:

> '...a lead-black thunderstorm cloud was observed moving toward the coast. Unexpectedly, ...an enormous gray trunk descended slowly to the surface of the sea from the clouds. As soon as it touched the sea, a column of foam and dust was lifted up. Then everything became one water column. The gigantic top gradually widened and menacingly approached the coast. It appeared as if the sea was connected to the sky and water poured up as in a strange hose.'[6] It lasted 19 minutes.

WHIRLPOOLS

What does the whirlpool known as *The Maelstrom of Saltstraumen* in Norway have in common with waterspouts/whirlwinds over large bodies of water? It is claimed to have the world's strongest current of any strait on flood tides (recorded at up to 41 kph), and is yet another extreme of nature for unsuspecting mariners.

Like waterspouts, such whirlpools may occur without significant warning and generate a deep and wide, funnel-like swirling mass of water ('vortex'). They have been described as 'spinning underwater tornadoes' by some.

Saltstraumen is a small strait three kilometres in length located about 10 kilometres from the nearest Norwegian town of Bodo near the Arctic Circle. Its narrow channel, 150 metres wide, connects the outer Saltfjorden (fjord), which is entirely open to the sea, with the large Skjerstad Fjord which is almost entirely sealed by land. The strait experiences exceptionally strong tidal currents, as up to 400 million cubic metres of seawater rushes between the fjords every six hours.[7]

The most powerful whirlpools or *maelstroms* form in this strait when the current flow is at its strongest. This may also be affected by strong winds or additional fresh water entering the fjords from surrounding mountains.

As the fast flowing seawater traverses the channel, opposing tidal currents collide and the destructive interaction creates powerful circular turbulence or 'eddies', which present at the surface as whirlpools. Such currents only cease briefly on the rising tide, giving ships but a short time to safely pass.[8]

The term maelstrom refers to the most violent or extraordinarily large whirlpools, as the name duly suggests. American poet and short-story writer Edgar Allan Poe eloquently describes the effect in his 1841 tale entitled *A Descent Into The Maelstrom*, as illustrated by the following excerpts about another unusual whirlpool at Moskstraumen off the coast of Norway:

> 'In five minutes the whole sea … was lashed into ungovernable fury … Here the vast bed of the waters, seamed and scarred into a thousand conflicting channels, burst suddenly into phrensied [frenzied] convulsion –heaving, boiling, hissing –gyrating in gigantic and innumerable vortices, and all whirling and plunging on to the eastward with a rapidity which water never elsewhere assumes except in precipitous descents …"the great whirlpool of the Maelstrom"…
>
> … When the stream is most boisterous, and its fury heightened by a storm, it is dangerous to come within a Norway mile of it. Boats, yachts, and ships have been carried away by not guarding against it before they were within its reach. It likewise happens frequently, that whales come too near the stream, and are overpowered by its violence; and then it is impossible to describe their howlings and bellowings in their fruitless struggles to disengage themselves.'[9]

Large whirlpools can also produce a loud roaring noise, caused by churning water rushing through the vortex at great speeds. The reverberation roar of one of the world's largest whirlpools, in the Strait of Corryvreckan off the coast of Scotland, can be heard from 16 kilometres away.[10]

In ancient bygone days, superstitious seafarers wondered if the screeching and booming sounds emanating from such violent whirlpools were 'giant undersea monsters'.[11] Various whirlpools elsewhere in the world may generate upwellings of the water, standing waves, smaller associated whirlpools and other chaotic side effects as the fast flowing tidal currents seethe and swirl around submerged rocks on the channel floor or sea bed of the strait.

As most of the world's significant whirlpool regions have been nautically charted over time for shipping purposes, large maritime vessels tend to avoid such perils. It is the unlucky smaller craft which are considerably more susceptible.

Whirlpools of Western Australia

In the remote West Kimberley coastal region of Western Australia where the gigantic tides are amongst the world's largest, and the variation in amplitude between high and low tides could peak between 11-12 metres, there is a rather unusual feature named Whirlpool Pass (Latitude 16°15′S, Longitude 123°30′E). It leads a convoluted five kilometre 'S' bend passage between three islands, and '... is only 0.2 mile (320 metres) wide at its narrowest part, and the tidal currents run with great rapidity through it, forming whirlpools, which restrict navigation only to slack water by small craft with local knowledge'.[12]

At times of peak tidal movements, currents in Whirlpool Passage, as it is known locally, are running in excess of 20 kph. Traversing Whirlpool Pass when the water is flowing at up to this speed, creating metre-deep whirlpools (or considerably deeper ones), and boils of rising water 10-20cm higher than the surrounding surface, can be quite a daunting experience.[13]

Another Australian passage further west, again between local islands and subject to whirlpools, is Escape Pass ((Latitude 16°25′S, Longitude 123°0′E). It is '... the shortest route into King Sound from the W [West]'.[14]

King Sound is a vast coastal inlet (145 kilometres in length and averaging 50 kilometres in width) that expands from the mouth of one of Australia's largest inland watercourses (Fitzroy River) into the Indian Ocean. King Sound's outer entrance from the ocean is flanked by clusters of islands, isles and innumerable reefs and shoals.

ON THE EDGE

Although Escape Pass located off Sunday Island, between Tallon Island and the reef system of Jackson Island, is deep with a minimum width of about 640 metres, its currents can also attain 20 kph on spring tides.[15]. The resultant whirlpools that form as the tide rips and rushes along this passage can be both spectacular and treacherous.

Figure 16: Escape Pass near King Rock, West Kimberley Coast, Australia (© Cygnet Bay Pearls)

Substantially further northwards along this coast is the ominously named Whirlpool Straits (estimated Latitude 15°10'S, Longitude 124°40'E), between Brunswick Bay and Saint George Bay in north-west Kimberley.

What makes this strait rather unusual is that at peak tidal flows, the seawater drains or fills three connected water bodies (Rothsay Water; Munster Water; and Saint George Basin, with its [freshwater] Prince Regent River).

The seafloor in this area is also extraordinarily variable in depth, representing the drowned undulations of the original hills (peaks) and valleys (troughs). When combined with a relatively large tidal range of greater than four metres, the result is '…creation of fast moving currents, great turbulence plus spectacular whirlpools and domed upwellings'. The turbulence is powerful enough to push larger powered vessels off-course.[16]

SPECTACULAR TIDES

Massive tidal movements ebbing and flowing twice daily are attributable to the gravitational pull of the moon and the sun, and are at their maximum when the earth, sun and moon are in alignment. This combined effect results in spring tides, representing the highest 'high tides' and the lowest 'low tides' possible in an area. When the earth is closest to the sun, such tidal changes are further increased.[17]

The world's largest tidal range occurs in the northern hemisphere, in the Bay of Fundy located between the Canadian provinces of New Brunswick and Nova Scotia. This tidal movement can approach an enormous 17 metres at the most inland part of the bay, excluding abnormal outside influences caused from storms and high winds.[18]

Like the Bay of Fundy, the Severn Estuary between England and Wales in the United Kingdom is also a wide-mouthed, long, shallow bay with a funnel shape. It sits at the mouth of four major rivers, resulting in a huge tidal range and extreme tide movement of up to 13 metres.[19]

In the southern hemisphere, the biggest tides are to be found on Australia's north-west coast around the port of Derby and in Collier Bay.[20] At 12 metres, the West Kimberley port of Derby in King Sound is acknowledged as having the highest tidal range of any Australian port.[21]

In Collier Bay, located further north-east along the rugged West Kimberley coast of Western Australia, physical oceanographic research studies have identified spring tidal ranges of 12 metres between high and low tides occur regionally.[22] Of course exceptionally high tides (known as King tides) that only occur twice annually will affect tidal speed. Tide speeds racing through the constricted entrance to the Walcott Inlet estuary located in Collier Bay could be as high as 28 km/hr.[23]

In Kimberley coastal regions such as Derby and Collier Bay, other factors also play a role influencing massive tides, including the shallow waters between islands and the shape and depth of the seafloor off the nearby coast. As the tidal forces from the deep ocean reach the relatively wide but shallow Continental Shelf, the tidal height or 'amplitude' becomes enlarged, and further enhanced by shallow waters around islands.[24]

As famous Scottish poet Robert Burns quoted in his 1790 poem *Tam o'Shanter*: 'Nae man can tether time nor tide' – time and tide wait for no man.[25]

Periodically, many unusual and often extreme tidal activities occur along select stretches of coast, assisted by the variable depth of seabed and many submerged reefs and submarine ridges. These contribute to constricting strong tidal currents, creating eddies and counter currents, as well as generating gigantic tidal convergence or 'ripplings' and 'overfalls'.

The Kimberley coast of Western Australia not only has exceptionally powerful tide movements, but also has 2,633 offshore islands (almost one third of the total 8,330 islands located within Australia's jurisdiction). Therefore there is a high concentration of islands in this area of sea.[26]

Consequently, there are many aquatic phenomena along this coast, and their locations have been given interesting names such as Tide Rip Islands, Hell's Gate, The Funnel, and the world famous 'Horizontal Waterfalls' at The Gaps in Talbot Bay.

The Tide Rip Islands, (also originally named as 'Tiderip Island', or *Nunba* by the local indigenous people),[27] are a small neighbouring group of three rocky, irregular and barren islands standing on a common reef. These tiny islands protruding 33-41m above sea level are located in the Sunday Strait – the main entrance to King Sound for the port of Derby.

They share this strait with shoals, isolated reefs, and several other islands of varying size.[28]

However, the Tide Rip Islands (Latitude 16°19'S, Longitude 123°19'E and nearby areas in particular are noted for strong and dangerous tidal currents that run with considerable velocity (up to 20 km/hr on spring tides), tidal rips, dangerous 'overfalls' in proximity to substantial rock outcrops, and precarious shallow channels. This coastal stretch of the Sunday Strait comes with sensible precautionary warnings to navigate any passage '…during daylight hours only, and preferably at the time of slack water'.[29]

The aptly named 'Horizontal Waterfalls' (Latitude 16°23′S, Longitude 123°58′E) are created when massive spring tides of up to 10 metres height difference pass through two consecutive narrow gaps in vertical towering sandstone strata [of the McLarty Range] in both rising and falling tidal situations.

At such peak times, the surging seawater so confined by the narrowest gap cascades through this entrance, resembling a spectacular waterfall in the ocean.[30]

English poet and writer John Masefield evokes the spirit of tides so well in the following excerpt from his 1902 seafarer's poem *Sea Fever*:

> '…I must go down to the seas again, for the call of the running tide
> Is a wild call and a clear call that may not be denied;
> And all I ask is a windy day with the white clouds flying,
> And the flung spray and the blown spume, and the sea-gulls crying…'[31]

UNSTABLE ATMOSPHERICS

'Everyone is familiar with storms. Storms happen when the stable conditions of the atmosphere have been disturbed … manifested by very strong winds and usually accompanied by rain or snow, thunder and lightning, and hail. The damage caused by storms can be total'.[1]

Storms are distinctive meteorological phenomena and can be as complex and large in scale as tornadoes/spouts and seasonal cyclones around the world. However, life-threatening land-based tornadoes and tropical cyclones/hurricanes/typhoons are not the subject of this book, simply because they would warrant an entire manuscript!

Storms may take many configurations, and result in not only damaging impact but also in transporting ground materials (vegetation, soil, sand and dust) and living matter. Extreme storms are decidedly the most destructive, such as many thunderstorms combined into one super-thunderstorm or smaller, more intense torrential storms or hailstorms.

UNSTABLE ATMOSPHERICS

Figure 17: Storm (© Shutterstock)

HAILSTORMS

In the right atmospheric conditions, when heated air rises rapidly and the water vapour it contains condenses at high altitude, frozen water forms and falls to earth. Hailstones formed at great altitude can attain enormous size when additional layers of ice are able to accumulate, thus increasing their weight.

Phenomenal sizes of hailstones have been recorded in the world at various times. A severe hailstorm on 30 April 1888 near Moradabad in Uttah Pradash, India, killed 246 people with hailstones as large as "goose eggs and oranges and cricket balls".[2]

In the 19th Century, there are recorded reports of hailstones varying in size between hen's eggs and baseballs, especially in the USA, with such gigantic hail sometimes creating small craters or simply deluging a neighbourhood.[3] In one extreme case, '… the hail [in the valley] was sufficient to form a layer 6ft [1.8m] deep and 10 acres [4 hectares] in area. In the steppe [flatland], hail killed six horses'.[4] Extreme hail damage to property can be catastrophic.

Australia's costliest natural disaster in the nation's insurance history was the exceptional Sydney supercell hailstorm in April 1999 that dropped an estimated 500,000 tonnes of hailstones in its path. Much of the hail was similar in size to tennis balls.[5]

The duration and severity of this hail and the frequent changes in storm direction wreaked considerable havoc along the east coast of New South Wales. The resultant total damage bill (including uninsured damages) for the storm was estimated to be around A$2.3 billion.[6] In spite of all this mayhem and destruction, there was only one fatality, when a person was struck by lightning.

ELECTRICAL STORMS

Electrical storms are probably just as unpredictable as hail storms and occasionally can develop without much warning. The electrical phenomena associated with lightning may simply arise on a calm, humid and overcast day, heralded acoustically by a booming clap of thunder but little rain. At other times, the lightning bolts emanate from billowing thunderstorm clouds to an almost constant drumming of thunder.

Extreme electrical storms with virtually continuous lightning strikes can be particularly daunting. In France in 2012, the longest duration lightning strike was recorded as lasting 7.74 seconds.[7]

Some parts of the world are known as "lightning hotspots" or the homes of "everlasting storms". Lake Maracaibo in north-western Venezuela and, to a lesser extent, the eastern Democratic Republic of the Congo, are recognised for having the highest number of lightning strikes per square kilometre. In that area of Venezuela, there are 1.2 million lightning flashes per annum. Both places have considerable precipitation and ideal humidity and atmospheric conditions for thunderstorm development.[8]

Who among us has ever been caught outdoors in the beginnings of a potentially ferocious electrical storm, perhaps with little advance warning?

Sometimes it simply starts with random flashes of crackling lightning far away in the distance. Only the ensuing acoustic signature of an ear-splitting roll of thunder startles you into acute awareness. A thunder clap that is so loud and ominous that it rattles nearby glass windows or crockery on the shelf. Thunder so loud that it sounds as if a grand piano has just fallen down a flight of stairs in the sky.

The level of your apprehension quickly escalates once you recognise that the lightning flashes are increasing in duration and intensity. Thoughts rapidly turn to seeking appropriate shelter, as so many options appear too risky, such as under large trees or near metallic towers and other prominent tall structures.

Then without any further indication, the storm clouds release a deluge of soaking rain and the startling lightning dissipates just as rapidly. Now thoughts turn to finding a suitable umbrella instead.

Your initial trepidation about actually being struck by a bolt of lightning is only offset by the estimation that such an encounter may release a mere one billion volts of electricity. Now that is a most impressive thought, and yet particularly daunting for anyone flying in an aircraft through such dramatic electrical atmospherics.

STORMS AT SEA

Storms at sea are traditionally named 'squalls' as they tend to be localised, develop suddenly, and dissipate just as quickly. They can be extremely violent, and mariners throughout history are wary of their concentrated destructive strength. It is quite possible for a squall to increase from no more than a slight breeze to a raging torrent in a matter of minutes, and then cease shortly afterwards.

Another feature of squalls at sea is the variety of phenomena that may be associated with them; intense freezing gusts of wind, driving rain, icy sleet and snow. Mayhem and turmoil follow for sailors, which is possibly why the word 'squall' also refers to 'a loud cry' [for help].

In March 1878, the English Royal Naval frigate *Eurydice* encountered a sudden and unexpected squall as it entered a bay, although the unusual and fierce tempest only lasted a few minutes. '… snow covered the horizon, changing day into night. The sea seethed with waves … 'Afterwards, there was no sign of the vessel, as it had capsized and sunk with all hands.[9]. This is still considered by many to be one of Britain's worst peace-time naval disasters, with the loss of 364 lives.[10]

Figure 18: Squall at Sea (© Shutterstock)

DUST STORMS AND SAND STORMS

Short-lived dustless storms as also known as squalls, whereas dust storms '…can have a duration of several days… cover thousands of kilometers, spreading hundreds of kilometers in width'.[11] In the case of large behemoth dust storms '… the height of the cloud [of dust] is 2 km or more and the sun's rays cannot be seen through it, often causing total darkness'.[12]

To effectively gauge the impact of such gargantuan storms, consider how much sand, soil and dust is transported.

On the afternoon of 14 April 1935 ('Black Sunday'), one of the worst black blizzards swept away topsoil across the Great Plains between Canada south to Texas in the USA. Day turned to night for many inhabitants, and 350 million tons [318 million tonnes] of topsoil was estimated to be displaced from the prairie area in the US.[13] These 'dark' storms envelop towns, cities and occasionally entire States.

By contrast, 'sandstorms' are relatively uncommon throughout the world compared to dust storms, and are typically found in regions of desert or vast tracts of aeolian dunes, such as the Sahara.

What is probably not commonly known is that violent sandstorms also generate enormous masses of finer suspended 'dust' particles that may extend to a height of one to two kilometres, whilst the relatively heavier, medium-coarse sand is actually transported by rolling and dragging in the form of mobile streams located very close to the ground.[14]

Sandstorms can easily be mistaken for dust storms. 'A typical sandstorm looks like a simple dense low cloud with a sharply defined upper surface, grazing the ground like a carpet … may reach a height of 2 m but generally it is less … where the sand contains no dust.'[15]

For those unfortunate people caught unaware in a sandstorm, the effect of being struck at body height by highly abrasive sand grains propelled at 20 m/sec (70 kph) and above can be devastating. These '…sand particles polish everything on the surface of the desert, create three-cornered sand dunes and destroy the hardest rocks on the surface of the earth. All this occurs on the surface'.[16] They may last a few hours or a few days.

SNOWSTORMS

Many countries in the northern hemisphere are familiar with snowstorms ('blizzards') or extreme snowfalls, sometimes inundating entire regions and States. These catastrophic storms can create the same kind of devastation and loss of life as occurs with tornadoes and cyclones/hurricanes/typhoons.

Exceptionally violent snowstorms in populated areas share common parameters – sub-zero freezing temperatures, icy gale-force gusty winds, excessive snowfall and a lingering duration of many days. Sometimes only the tops of telegraph poles and the roofs of houses remain above the snowline. Railroads, highways, widespread livestock and even entire villages may become buried. In March 1966 in the central States of the USA, just such an exceptional storm formed snow drifts 10 -12 m deep.[17]

In more remote areas, even harsher conditions may prevail, affecting the few hardy inhabitants, visiting tourists or extreme trekkers venturing through such regions. In the extensive Alps mountain range of Central Europe 'enormous clouds of dry snow' may be lifted by the strong prevailing winter winds to such an extent that travel is not possible due to poor visibility.

Furthermore, these ominous snow clouds can gather dust, sand and even fine chips of stone, and the strength of the storm is such that light structures can be destroyed and roofs can be torn from buildings. The locals often place rocks on roofs to prevent them being blown away.[18] Trekking through such mountainous areas during the colder months is for the cautious, particularly with respect to potential avalanches.

The polar regions (Antarctica and the Arctic) could easily be classified as the areas subject to the worst snowstorms, in terms of both frequency and strength of wind. With so much land permanently covered by ice in Antarctica and in Greenland, the wind tends to carry only ice and snow.

Storms can last for months and temperatures always remain well below zero. The highest wind speeds recorded in Antarctica were at Dumont d'Urville station in July 1972 and reached 327 kph.[19]

The following frightening sentiment reported in 1848 by local sailors about a cold torrential wind in the Arctic region succinctly portrays the harsh reality of such storms:

> ' ... The inconceivable strength of the wind with fierce gusts, hard frost, total darkness in daytime, small needles of frozen dust in the air, the hum, rustling, whistle –all were mixed up in one chaotic condition as if it was the harbinger of the destruction of the world. This continued for more than three days without any change in strength'.[20]

IT'S RAINING CATS, DOGS, TOADS AND FISH

Intense storms with severe updraft air jets and very powerful vortices have been recorded throughout much of human history as having transported an endless array of animals and other living species. The familiar adage of 'raining cats and dogs' is not that far from the truth after all.

However, the flight of dogs and cats plucked up by passing storms and unceremoniously dumped to earth in rain some distance away is relatively rare. Conversely, the transportation of smaller, lightweight aquatic animals, such as fish, frogs and toads is relatively common, commencing by rain with fish observed as early as the 7th century (689 A.D.) in Saxony.[21]

The type of fish wrenched from pools, small lakes and paddy fields varies considerably, as does the subsequent transportation distance. In 1900, a thunderstorm accompanied by a heavy downpour and strong wind near Providence, Rhode Island, USA, inundated a man with only freshwater fish 5 -12 cm in length. This 'rain of fish' was concentrated over a small area of one quarter acre (0.4 hectare). They were so prolific that the fish were subsequently displayed in store shopwindows as an unusual catch.[22]

In England in 1666 and far from the sea or any lakes, after the rain from thunderstorm cloud had ceased, the ground was ' … completely covered with various types of small fish of finger size… weighed about a bushel (40 kg) and were later sold in the market.[23]

Rain with frogs and toads in their thousands have also been frequently reported, although probably have gone largely unnoticed compared with the unusual phenomenon of live fish landing after rain. An amusing outcome to such 'rain of fish' was the discovery by an Englishman in 1830 of fish in his rain gauge, perhaps signifying the extent of fish falling from the sky on that particular day.

THE LONG HIKE

'I love to go a-wandering,
Along the mountain track,
And as I go, I love to sing,
My knapsack on my back…

…I wave my hat to all I meet, |
And they wave back to me,
And blackbirds call so loud and sweet
From ev'ry green wood tree.

High overhead, the skylarks wing,
They never rest at home
But just like me, they love to sing,
As o'er the world we roam.

Oh, may I go a-wandering
Until the day I die!
Oh, may I always laugh and sing,
Beneath God's clear blue sky!'[1]

ON THE EDGE

The selected original lyrics from the song *The Happy Wanderer* composed by Florenz Friedrich Sigismund in the 19th century seems timeless, and so does hiking. Who has not ventured along a mountain goat track or hilly trail in search of how far it reaches?

Who has not wandered aimlessly along a country lane or quiet path following a meandering stream and thought this must lead somewhere, only to discover that it does not? Probably deep within most of us there will always be that motivation, that curiosity, that spark of interest to find what is around the next bend, over that hill or across that ravine.

Most people are natural-born explorers and usually enjoy the exhilaration and personal challenge of finding new places to visit, even if it may mean hiking for kilometres. When new physical obstacles present to us, we simply bypass them or perhaps trudge onwards regardless. For the few that relent and find the trek just too difficult, they will never know what they have missed.

Figure 19: One More Bridge to Cross (© Shutterstock)

THE LONG HIKE

Weather is certainly the most unforgiving curse of hikers – they may be drenched by passing showers, chilled by driving icy-cold winds and freezing sleet, frightened by random lightning strikes, choked by gusty dust storms or suffer sweltering tropical heat and humidity. Then there are the ancillary side effects of such weather, such as muddy trails, swollen streams/rivers, occasional rock falls and pesky insect swarms.

The company of other hikers is always a comfort, unless of course they are travelling in the opposite direction, perhaps due to the immense difficulties already encountered ahead. Who really needs company when you have Mother Nature to comfort you? The four elements of Earth, Air, Fire and Water, as well as the wide open spaces (Space – the fifth element), are certainly great comforters, until you falter.

Being in the outdoors 'at one with nature' is most certainly satisfying and enlightening, so long as those pesky insects leave you alone at night. Hiking any designated major long-distance trail from end to end in a single trip is for those with the physical stamina and free time to complete extraordinary distances on foot. Some perhaps temporarily deviate from the designated route at convenient stop-overs for sustenance and recuperation.[2]

The world's longest hiking route, Canada's The Great Trail, which opened in late 2017, is 23,921 kilometres long and stretches from coast to coast spanning the entire country. It took a monumental 25 years to establish, linking more than 400 existing community-based trails into a single massive network.[3]

In the USA, the Continental Divide (National Scenic) Trail traverses five US States, stretching 4,989 km between Mexico and Canada, whilst the Pacific Crest (National Scenic) Trail extends 4,279 km along the entire length of the west coast, closely aligned with the Sierra Nevada and Cascade mountain ranges.[4]

To hike the full length of the longer Continental Divide Trail end to end can take about six months to complete in a single trip, though the time taken is highly dependent on the difficulty of the routes selected, the hiker's stamina and determination, and a myriad of other factors.

ON THE EDGE

For some, it is a further challenge to just complete all the major long distance trails. The world has a considerable number of hiking trails rated by hikers as being extremely tough to complete. Most are located in various mountainous regions, such as in Hawaii, Spain, South Africa, China, and in countries around the Himalayas.

Figure 20: Rugged Hiking Trail (© Shutterstock)

THE LONG HIKE

South America certainly has many challenging hiking trails, and it is in the Peruvian Andes that one can face some particularly daunting hikes. If you prefer remote trekking through mountainous terrain semi-shrouded in mist and clouds, crossing steep canyons and spectacular ravines, and savouring majestic panoramic views, the physical hardships may be well worth the effort.

Of course a considerable part of hiking over long distance is finding a place to spend the night. For a refreshing night's sleep, it is best to select a safe site most protected from the intensity of the inclement weather and any inquisitive wildlife likely to intrude.

For those selecting suitable overnight camping sites in various remote or secluded parts of Britain, there can be many daunting challenges, most notably from the weather.

The coastal extremities of Britain may be subject to the cold, damp sea air and soaking foggy mists prevalent in certain seasons, whilst incessant rain or perhaps merely brief showers driven by the wind may persist at other times.

The regional winds from the Arctic north howling in from across the Atlantic Ocean, the North Sea or the Irish Sea and onto the coastal hinterland could definitely add more discontent for any hardy trekker. A tent may not withstand such weather, or worse still, it may leak rainwater throughout the night hours.

Mud and slush are not definitely not the friend of a hiker. For the far more adventurous trekker, seeking the security of a cave or tunnel to spend the night might be more appropriate.

Caves can be rather peculiar places in which to reside overnight, particularly if already inhabited by miscellaneous insects, such as mosquitoes, hornets and spiders; or perhaps reptiles like snakes or lizards; even bats that may frequent such nocturnal spaces. This is where a hiker's torch proves invaluable.

Once it has been confirmed that the selected cave is not already inhabited, the next obligatory step is to ensure that it is reasonably secure from rockfall, flooding and other forms of personal entrapment.

Caves offer quite a sanctuary from inclement weather and cold drafts, although the air quality can sometimes appear 'stuffy', and for some hikers, small caverns may appear rather claustrophobic for space. A cave or tunnel's overall size and depth of penetration inside a rockface or cliff may also result in the contained air seeming extremely 'chilly' during the night. If all these factors do not concern the hiker, then a good night's sleep is reasonably assured.

The moorland dales (valleys) and flatlands of North Yorkshire in Britain are another particularly notable area for hiking and camping, especially in the colder months of the year. The 'moors' cover 1,430 square kilometres and are one of the largest expanses of such moorland in the United Kingdom.[5]

In the cooler seasons, the weather can fluctuate from unsettled and windy to cold chilling spells with variable periods of snowfall. The area gets much more snow on average than other parts of the country.[6] Now combine this unpredictable and often bleak weather with the exposed terrain for a hiker seeking suitable shelter from the rain, cold winds and sometimes snowfalls. There are plentiful small rocky outcrops scattered throughout the landscape, but often too inadequate for much camping protection.

There are also innumerable peat bogs containing icy water or sodden mud to avoid or jump over, and substantial tuffs of prickly heather to irritate the skin. Although the moors have more dry days than those with rain per annum, this does not account for the ethereal mists arising from the moss bogs or areas of low-lying marshlands, or sea mists blown by prevailing onshore winds. For those enjoying such camping, it most certainly provides many personal challenges.

THE LONG HIKE

STAIRS

Not quite the extraordinary length of a major trekking trail, but nonetheless still a rigorous and sometimes daunting test for some hikers are the various worldwide outdoor stairs constructed for access on mountainsides, in ravines, beside waterfalls, on temples and in some cities.

The world's longest outdoor stairs are listed by the official Guinness Book of Records as the Niesenbahn Stairway that is built on the slopes of the pyramid-shaped Mount Niesen in the Swiss Alps. This is a service stairway for Niesenbahn funicular railway, and comprises a massive 11,674 steps.[7]

The 3.4 kilometre inclined stairs are built beside the 'Niesen mountain railway' that terminates near the summit at 2,363 m above sea level, attaining a staggering average gradient of 55 per cent. Climbing these steps to the top would be '… the equivalent to climbing the Empire State Building [New York, USA] 7 times'.[8]

While the extreme length of staircase is only used by service personnel and is usually closed to the public, it is opened one day per annum for a challenging endurance race for up to 500 participants. Given its elevated mountainside location, the Niesen stairs are also subject to snow and passing cloud.

For outdoor stairs comprising only wooden steps, Norway's Flørli Stairs at Lysefjord has 4,444 of them, 'often considered to be one of the longest wooden staircases in the world'.[9]

The staircase was originally used by maintenance teams for two industrial pipes traversing the mountain from a hydroelectric power station, since abandoned and no longer in use. Hikers who successfully complete the long trek on the wooden steps are amply rewarded by the outstanding fjord views from a height of 740 metres above sea level.[10]

If the trekker does not require the challenge of an enormous number of steps or a mountainous location, then possibly Ukraine's Potemkin Stairs ('the Giant Staircase') in the city of Odessa may be worthwhile. This staircase only has 192 steps and extends for 142 metres over a height of 27 metres, but is quite an optical illusion appearing of greater length.[11]

The bottom steps are constructed wider than those at the top, and when looking down from above, only the landings remain visible to the naked eye and no steps at all. From the bottom, only the steps remain visible.[12]

Figure 21: Staircase beside Devil's Cauldron (© Shutterstock)

When steps are not a uniform width, it takes considerably longer to traverse them. This is not concern with the 444 Steps (Escalera) located in the old Las Peñas neighbourhood of Guayaquil in Ecuador. A leisurely pace would suffice along these steps to the hilltop of Santa Ana, overlooking the colourfully painted houses (many 400-years-old), art galleries and artist studios of the district.

A far more extreme outdoor staircase is located in the western foothills of the Ecuadorian Andes. These steep and almost always slippery steps are adjacent to the spectacular 80 metre high *Pailón del Diablo* waterfall - translated as the 'Cauldron of the Devil'. It is situated on the Rio Pastaza which is a tributary of the upper Amazon River Basin.

If the waterfall's name is not enough to warn hikers, they're sure to notice that the steps are slippery due to the constant mist and overspray from the nearby falls. These stone steps are comprised of smooth oversized pebbles that provide little traction for the trekker, and yield an optical illusion from above that the stairs are one continuous slide to the bottom.[13]

Because the well-built steps in the vertical cliffs are perpetually in shade, the illusion is that they appear to blend together, thus resembling a rock slide instead of a stairway.[14] Safety handrails are available and always recommended.

SKRAPING

Arduous recreational trekking across particularly difficult terrain has been emerging as one of the newest extreme sports. Adventure racing on foot, or Škraping (pronounced: sh'kraping), has grown in popularity since its inception in Croatia in 2006.[15]

The term Škraping derives from the word Škrapa in Dalmation dialect, meaning 'sharp rock', and there is plenty of jagged, rough terrain involved in this sporting discipline.

This form of trekking involves crossing and sometimes free climbing (without equipment) sharp rocky outcrops of the landscapes, as well as traversing any local paths or dense vegetation by open-space orienteering to complete the trek in the shortest possible time. This involves a combination of walking, jumping and climbing skills with a distinctly competitive spirit, including the challenge of just being able to walk over such sharp rocks.[16]

Pašman is one of the biggest islands (63.3 square kilometres[17]) in the Zadar Archipelago, situated south of Zadar off the coast of the Adriatic Sea in Croatia, and also the site of an annual international Škraping race. The island has an indented shoreline with a karst topography of limestone rock providing the ideal setting of razor-sharp, jagged rocks on the coastline.[18]

Pašman Island's lack of arranged paths and the richness of untouched and unarranged parts of karst relief forms which are abundant on this island, are favourable for this type of "walk".[19] Traversing the abundant limestone ledges that line the island at sea-level provides a further challenge for trekkers.

The substantially larger island of Cres in the Adriatic Sea to the north of Zadar also has rugged razor sharp limestone rock that provides for challenging climbing conditions along parts of its foreshore.

Figure 22: Climbing Rock on the Island of Cres, Croatia

Editorial credit: rkl_foto/Shutterstock.com

Croatia's Paklenica National Park (95 square kilometres) is the premier climbing area for Škrapers, with deep canyons, vertiginous peaks and hundreds of routes along the steep canyon walls. The first challenge is to overcome the many jagged rock formations.[20]

EXTREME ANIMALS

The world has a plethora of animals with unusual habits, ambiguous traits and peculiar appearances. My selection only represents a minute proportion of these amazing animals. However, at least this will provide a glimpse at the extremes nature displays, and will give an insight into how such life forms can be so markedly diverse.

BILBIES

Let's start with one of the smallest animals: a soil burrowing native marsupial of Australia somewhat resembling an odd-looking bandicoot with oversized legs. This little character remains a rare and endangered species. Bilbies (*Macrotis lagotis*), known as greater bilbies, are desert dwelling marsupials of most distinctive appearance.

Their bodies of soft, silky fur, long pointy muzzles/snouts and oversized hairless ears have earned them the unusual comical title of 'rabbit-eared bandicoots'. Their slender, long hind legs resemble those of a kangaroo.¹ They also have an exceptionally long tail at around 29 centimetres or twice their body length, and are renowned for digging extensive burrows.

Figure 23: The Greater Bilby (© Shutterstock)

If such a diverse description was not enough, bilbies live a solitary nocturnal existence in arid to semi-arid regions, and yet all of their attributes serve practical purposes. Those gigantic manoeuvrable and flexible ears '…allow a portion of them to remain above ground level when they [bilbies] are digging so they can hear predators approaching'.²

Their long hind legs, strong forearms and powerful claws are perfect burrowing tools. Their snout provides a well-honed sense of smell for foraging, whilst their 48 teeth and long, sticky and slender tongue are excellent for devouring insects.³ Most remarkably, these amazing little creatures are persistent survivors against all odds. However, they are preyed upon by foxes and feral cats, and continue to remain an endangered species of native wildlife.⁴

WOMBATS

Another shy and solitary marsupial, but with a rather rotund physique is the common wombat (*Vombatus ursinus*). This sturdy, short-legged and relatively muscular character with a stubby tail almost resembles a small bear walking on all fours. It may even appear to be relatively cuddly, given how deceptively slowly it waddles along with an awkward gait. However, wombats can accelerate very quickly over short distances if threatened, sometimes even bowling over a predator. They are also most adept at deep burrowing below ground, excavating an extensive network of burrows.

Three distinctive qualities make this tough little critter (growing to about one metre in length and up to 35 kg in weight) highly unusual: their rear end/rump, their droppings/scats and their food. The wombat characteristically uses its large and toughened rump as a physical defence against attack by predators. It is composed mostly of cartilage [dense connective body tissue of rubber-like padding] and thus is resistant to bites and scratches.

A wombat's droppings are uniquely cube-shaped and usually left on rocks or other high places where they can be easily seen. They act as markers for each wombat's territory and are important for night navigation, as wombats can detect them with their keen sense of smell. The cubic shape apparently restricts the droppings falling of these vantage points and being lost in the surrounding soil.[5]

Wombats are herbivores ('vegetarians'), preferring mostly various grasses, plant roots, herbs, shrubs and even bark for their diets. As a result of gnawing on such tough vegetation, their rodent-like front teeth become particularly sharp and should be avoided in any confrontation. They may appear slow and cumbersome to the unwary, but get out of their way once they really get moving.

Figure 24: The Common Wombat (© Shutterstock)

THREE-TOED SLOTHS

There is another animal that is considered by many to be easily the world's slowest, and this is the arboreal ('tree-dwelling') sloth, and the most common species would be the brown-throated, three-toed sloth (*Bradypus variegatus*).

Perhaps rather unkindly, these distinctly unusual characters were dubbed 'the unready ones' during the 18th century, and were subsequently described by English author Oliver Goldsmith in 1825 as '... an incompleted work of nature'.[6] These descriptions probably stem from the sloth's incredibly slow pace of life. They spend much of their lives either hanging upside down by their long curved claws or reclining safely camouflaged high in the tree canopies of the tropical rainforests of Central and South America.

Everything about these herbivores is slow. Due to their low rate of metabo-

ON THE EDGE

lism, they only feed gradually, very slowly digesting the foliage of certain trees and vines (mainly), as well as berries and insects (for some species). Sloths have large multi-chambered stomachs and an ability to tolerate strong chemicals from the foliage they eat. When they do briefly return to the ground once per week, it is to pass their waste products.[7]

They only move when essential, preferring to hang from branches or perch in the forks of trees. They rarely remain on the ground, where they lack something to grasp and thus become relatively helpless and most vulnerable to predators.

The deliberate and thoughtfully slow movements of sloths are considered to be an unusual environmental adaption to their surroundings. Their subtle body coloration enables them to blend intimately with the natural foliage, assisted by the growth of host algae that may form in the fur of their shaggy coat. In fact, they move so slowly that communities of moths, beetles, mites and other parasitic insects cohabit with them, developing small ecosystems in their fur.[8]

These leaf-eating, hairy, lethargic mammals with long limbs, have facial features that appear to be almost human, including flat, rounded faces, tiny ears and sad eyes.[9] As a consequence, sloths will remain adorable and special in so many fascinating ways with few comparable peers.

CHEETAHS

For the world's fastest land-based animal over relatively short distances of about 200 metres, the cheetah is the top cat. This highly-tuned sprinter eventually reaches speeds of around 96-98 kph and is able to increase speed four times faster than most human beings. Nature has provided a loose and rangy slender build, a highly flexible spine and claws that even after retracted continue to provide additional ground traction when accelerating.[10]

This speedster only has very limited endurance and relies upon its stalking ability to slowly creep up on its prey without detection, and its agility in stopping quickly as the chase proceeds. However, it can also be vulnerable to other predatory competitors as the cheetah's speed is severely curtailed if injured, and its strength does not match its agility.[11] It might be 'fleet of foot', but certainly is not invincible.

POLAR BEARS

Speed and agility are not as important to one of the world's largest carnivores ('flesh-eaters'), and possibly amongst the most dangerous animals on our planet, the polar bear (*Ursus maritimus*) or 'maritime/ice bear'. The adult male grows to an enormous 2.4 -3 m in total height, weighs between 350 kg -700 kg and averages around 400 kg or greater in different regions.[12] This is a marine mammal and native to the remote circumpolar Arctic, encompassing Canada, Alaska, Russia, Greenland and parts of Norway.

Its preferred habitat is the Arctic sea-ice, which provides suitable access to its targeted prey of predominantly seals. Such adaptability to the dangerous and uncompromising sea pack-ice that may mobilise without much warning is certainly an indicator of this animal's keen survival instincts. Polar bears are perfectly adapted to walking on ice and snow, as well as swimming in near-freezing waters.

The polar bear's claws are a reasonable example of this adaptability. These are relatively short and stocky compared to those of other species of bears, perhaps to assist in gripping heavy prey (seals) and ice.[13] The claws are deeply scooped on the underside and thus well suited to the digging of ice.

This bear is also undaunted about prolonged swims in the freezing water, propelling itself with its large forepaws and aided by the buoyancy provided by its copious body fat.[14] In fact, there have been documented recordings of bears swimming for days over considerable distances to reach ice far from land.[15]

So what other qualities make this magnificent animal such an extraordinary example of life's extremes? Significantly, the polar bear has an incredibly well-developed sense of smell, being able to detect seals 1.6 kilometres away and buried under one metre of snow.[16] This acute sense of smell has considerable additional benefits, including tracking any cubs that may have wandered away, or sensing other animals that may be competitors or prey.

A polar bear's 'white' fur coat only appears to be white to us. The outer layer of long, coarse hairs are hollow and mostly transparent, so the coat optically reflects and scatters visible light. This effect creates a perfect camouflage whilst living on the sea ice and ice-bound terrains, although the fur does fade to yellow with aging. The hollow central core of these outer hairs is also able to '… allow solar energy to be absorbed by the bear through its skin', thus assisting in keeping it warm.[17] However, the thinner, shorter hairs of the bear's thick plush undercoat are not hollow, but are also colourless.

One similarity that polar bears share with the bulky wombat is a lumbering gait when walking, but do not be fooled. This sturdy bear is quite capable of brief spurts of speed, when the situation demands. When sprinting, they can reach up to 40 km/h for short distances.[18]

Unfortunately, this unique species of 'white bear' remains a particularly vulnerable species due to a number of factors, including global warming. However, it will always remain a very important animal to the indigenous peoples of the region.

THE AUSTRALIAN KELPIE (A SPECIAL BREED OF *CANIS LUPUS FAMILIARIS*)

Now for a special animal so very close to many people's hearts. The Australian Kelpie certainly has it all. If ever a canine thought like a person and behaved accordingly, it would have to be this dog species.

EXTREME ANIMALS

Figure 25: The Australian Kelpie (© Shutterstock)

To think like a human is difficult enough for any animal, but not for this species. It seems almost natural behaviour. With the simple single lick of its tongue, the kelpie informs its owner that it is hungry. No more is necessary. It is direct yet salient communication: 'Feed me!'. If it is time for a daily walk with its owner, the kelpie positions itself appropriately and looks forlornly straight at its owner. Well, what is the delay today?

Bedtime is even more interesting for most kelpie owners. As an intelligent species, the kelpie expects the optimum available comfort when retiring to bed, including clean bedding, a comfortable cushion, doggie basket or cosy set of blankets, and a safe retreat away from other irritating dogs.

If this animal is employed as a farm's working dog – mustering or droving sheep or other likewise arduous tasks – he won't need a walk after an exhausting day's workload but will retire straight to bed after an appropriately satisfying meal. The special attributes these dogs possess include their intense determination to understand even simple instructions and unwavering loyalty to their owners.

Of course, enjoying the benefits of living with kind humans rate highest on the doggie scale. Kelpies' most endearing quality is without doubt the instinctive ability to anticipate their owners' thoughts – a dog's intuition. If ever a canine species is intimately aligned to humans, it must be the Australian Kelpie.

The name kelpie originates from Scottish folklore and translates as 'the spirit of the waters', with origins from collie-type working dog breeds that were brought to Australia in the late 19th century for their capabilities of herding sheep. As Australia's emerging rural population of merino sheep expanded significantly, so the need progressively increased for such an athletic and rugged species suited to working vast 'mobs' often in harsh climatic conditions over considerable distances.

Remarkably, these highly active dogs may be required to cover 50-60 kilometres in a single day. The crossing of a few such imported Scottish working dogs eventually produced the rather distinctive kelpie that became one of the earliest registered dog breeds in the country in 1902.[19]

This dog has been variously described as an independent quick-thinker, a diligent and fanatical 'workaholic', an extremely active breed and most favourably, said to be worth many men [when working sheep]. A contemporary definition of *kelpie* is 'an Australian breed of sheepdog with a smooth coat and erect ears, originally developed from Scottish collies'.[20] Somehow, I feel that a kelpie is far more than simply a sheepdog with pointy ears.

THE PLATYPUS

For possibly one of the strangest mammals on our planet, the semi-aquatic platypus (*Ornithorhynchus anatinus*) immediately catches your attention.

EXTREME ANIMALS

At first appearance, it resembles a beaver with a similar small furry body and wide flat tail, but it has a large and rubbery nose akin to a 'duck's bill'.

It also has webbed feet similar to a duck to assist this proficient swimmer through the water. Platypuses can be found in small streams, rivers, swamps, some shallow freshwater lakes and on river banks. They can also swim quickly underwater for long distances.

Figure 26: The Platypus (© Shutterstock)

This mammal's snout/bill is unique in many ways, serving not only as an effective tool to dislodge any prospective aquatic prey from river beds, but also as acting as an electrical sensor covered with a myriad of minute receptors. The platypus swims with its eyes shut, and changes in the electrical field help to guide it.[21]

This shy and reclusive animal produces its young by laying eggs, just to be different from all other extant mammals (with the exception of the echidna [spiny anteater]). Finally, if this was not enough to distinguish this remarkable character, the male platypus appears deceptively passive yet is armed with a poisonous pointy spur on its hind ankles to fend off competitors or to protect itself if otherwise threatened.[22]

This bundle of surprises that is a cross somewhere between a beaver, an otter and a duck, and waddles like reptile, exhibits all the credentials of a distinctly bizarre animal.

CURIOUS AVIANS

CROWS

Of the myriad of curious birds that inhabit our planet, the common Australian black Torresian crow (*Corvus orru*) surely provides a suitable benchmark for unusual avian behaviour.

Considered by some to have the mental capacity of a typical seven-year-old child, the clever crow is able to accurately mimic many other bird sounds and readily adapts to living amongst humans.

It even has a particularly irritating, loud and raucous croaking call ('caw'), and crows appear to communicate almost like chattering people.

This well versed 'language' probably provides a satisfactory communication medium for crows, who recognise many familiar objects and people's faces without any trouble. They are one of nature's avian rascals when it comes to opportunistic scavenging.

ON THE EDGE

Figure 27: Enigmatic Crow (© Shutterstock)

WILLIE WAGTAILS

In stark contrast to the crow is a significantly smaller and very cute bird known as the willie wagtail (*Rhipidura leucophrys*). The willie (or willy) wagtail is a contradiction in terms. It grows to only 19-22 cm in length, with a long fanned tail of 10-11 cm. However, this perching 'chatty' little bird comes with a distinctive flair for being aggressive, fearless and territorial. Its diverse range of bird calls include a rather alarming, harsh and militant whistling sound (rapid *chit-chit-chit-chit*) that is capable of harassing and scaring away much larger avians, such as crows and kookaburras. However, this is only part of its extreme repertoire.

This bird's survival success is really due to its characteristic flying habit that is so different to others. The willie wagtail is almost always on the move and is rarely still for more than a few moments during daylight hours. It runs, walks and hops with its tail usually held elevated. When pausing, the tail is constantly waved from side to side and up and down.[1]

Even while perching, it will flick its tail from side to side, twisting about looking for prey. The clever use of its enormous fantail provides considerable aerodynamic advantages as illustrated: 'It beats its wings deeply in flight, interspersed with a swift flying dip. It characteristically wags its tail upon landing after a short dipping flight'.[2]

This intriguing behaviour then really accelerates as this tiny bird forages for food on the ground. By swinging its tail from side to side or wagging it up or down while hopping, perhaps combined with wing flashing, the insect population that it pursues become sufficiently active and prone to capture.

The wagtails' 'dance' movements are intended to startle and confuse the insect prey by using changes in light intensity (shadows and movement) as the daily tools of trade.[3]

There is no mercy shown for the prey. The wagtail beats large insects senseless and strips other flying insects of their wings before consuming them.[4]

What is particularly fascinating about this pocket-sized dynamo is that during strong wind gusts it can be seen in various complex airborne positions. The sight of a highly agile bundle of feathers, being unceremoniously blown backwards and upside down, and thence cart-wheeling away into the distance is a sight to behold.

Not even the versatile wagtail can always resist the extreme forces of weather. Nonetheless, this intriguing and tricky little character remains in the top ten of Australia's favourite bird as voted by public poll.[5]

ON THE EDGE

THE BLUE-FOOTED BOOBY

For an avian that truly produces some interesting dance moves, the blue-footed booby (*Sula nebouxii*) combines a distinctive style of bopping with its bright blue legs and large webbed feet.

Figure 28: The Blue-Footed Booby (© Shutterstock)

This booby is a large marine bird native to subtropical and tropical regions of the eastern Pacific Ocean, with approximately one half of all breeding pairs nesting on the Galápagos Islands.[6] Males conduct an elaborate mating ritual by lifting their teal-blue feet up and down while strutting before the female. The males with the bluest feet are considered more attractive by the females.[7]

It is all about the quality of the high-step strutting routine. The name booby comes from the Spanish word *bobo* ("stupid", "foolish", or "clown") because the blue-footed booby is, like other seabirds, clumsy on land. Combining this ritualistic high-stepping feet stamping and strutting routine with frequent pointing of their heads skywards certainly produces an unusual dance effect similar to 'bopping'.[8]

A further distraction to the entire process is the blue-footed boobies' communication capability: they make raucous or polysyllabic grunts or shouts and thin whistling noises. The males of the species have been known to throw up their heads and whistle at passing, flying females. There's never a dull moment when these characters get started.

However, there is nothing clumsy about their fish hunting techniques, with these birds 'plunge diving' headfirst like arrows from heights of 10-100 m at about 97 km/h and reaching depths of 25 m below the water surface. They operate in large flocks like a well-drilled squadron of flyers, all diving in unison into the shoals of fish.[9]. Such agility, speed and precision at sea more than compensates for their apparent clumsiness on land.

BIRDS-OF-PARADISE AND QUETZALS

Elaborate manoeuvres and fanciful mating rituals may suit some birds, but when your tail feather is three times your body length, who needs all that exertion? The ribbon-tailed astrapia (*Astrapia mayeri*) or Shaw Mayer's astrapia is a species of bird-of-paradise endemic to the central highlands of Papua New Guinea, and (the male) has the longest tail feathers in comparison with body size of any other bird species in the world. It can grow to more than one metre.

The King of Saxony bird-of-paradise (*Pteridophora alberti*) from the mountainous forests of Papua New Guinea also has extraordinarily long plumage, but on its head. The elongated head plumes up to 50 cm in length resemble a feathery-leafed fern. These ornamental brow plumes are scalloped and appear so bizarre protruding from the bird as to seem almost fake, particularly when shaken back and forth.

To exceed such obvious attributes, the Guatemalan resplendent quetzal (*Pharomacrus moccino*) has large decorative and brilliant tail feathers, as well as a brightly coloured plumage of iridescent green or golden-green with a red belly. This stunning natural colour and the elongated glistening emerald-green tail feathers of the breeding male are considered by many to illustrate the immense beauty of the quetzal.

It is also recognised as the national bird of Guatemala,[10] and has the national currency named in its honour.[11] Glamorous plumage and long elaborate tail feathers are certainly a great combination.

THE RHINOCEROS HORNBILL

The rhinoceros hornbill (*Buceros rhinoceros*) is one of the world's largest forest-dwelling hornbills. It has a prominent golden-yellow horn ('casque') on top of its beak, giving it a rhinoceros-like appearance. This impressive helmet-like ornamentation is reflective of prehistoric hadrosaurids [duck-billed dinosaurs] from more than 60 million years ago.[12]

Although distinctive in appearance, the upturned hollow horn is thought be most practical as a resonating chamber for amplifying the bird's honking calls over considerable distances. Unusually, these calls resemble sounds like hooting and even laughter due to the shape of the helmeted casque. 'Hoooonk, hooonk…' resounded throughout the forest canopy and everyone paid attention.[13]

THE KING VULTURE

The king vulture (*Sarcoramphus papa*) is an enormous raptor with a wing span of up to two metres. It is also the third largest of the New World vultures, and found in Central and South America. However, this unusual 'king of the vultures' has some very fascinating facial features, including an absence of eyelashes and concentric circles for eyes.

Figure 29: The King Vulture (© Shutterstock)

In vivid contrast to the vulture's predominantly white plumage and dark tail feathers, its head and neck are bald, with highly variable skin colours of red and purple on the head, vivid orange on the neck and yellow on the throat.[14] The skin is wrinkled and folded, with an irregular, orange-bright red, fleshy caruncle ('wattle')/outgrowth drooping across its orange and black beak.[15] This bird has it all when it comes to an exotic look.

Notwithstanding that the king vulture's ultra-strong beak and long, thick (albeit blunt) claws are excellent tools for the one of the world's largest scavengers, its unusual upper body certainly make quite a statement. Another weird thing about this bird is that it lacks an effective vocal organ, thereby restricting it to low croaking and wheezing sounds, and to beak-snapping noises when threatened.[16]

THE GOULDIAN FINCH

So what does the king vulture have in common with possibly one of Australia's smallest birds: the gouldian finch (*Erythrura gouldiae*) also known as the rainbow finch? This incredibly colourful little beauty has a black, red or yellow head; body markings of green, red, yellow and black; and a distinctive light mauve to purple breast. It is almost a patchwork quilt of vivid colouration.

With such a magnificent, richly coloured plumage somewhat resembling a rainbow, these small finches are a stand-out in the avian community and are a splendid sight to human observers.[17] They do share something else in common with the king vulture.

Unlike similar birds to the finch, such as the variously coloured native budgerigars, or the larger parrots that may actually talk and enjoy the company of people, the gouldian finch does neither, preferring its own self-sufficiency. This finch is probably best described as an elegant bird who chooses its own path in life, preferring to live in the wild. Likewise, the vulture prefers its own company or small family groups.

FEARSOME SWIMMERS

The world's seas, oceans and other tidal bodies of water are home to an extreme diversity of creatures intent upon devouring their prey.

THE TIGER SHARK

Well over 400 species of sharks have been identified to date on this planet, and one in particular – the tiger shark – has quite a reputation for its ferocity and agility, and is second only to the terrifying and massive great white shark (*Carcarodan carcharias*) in number of reported attacks on humans. Its large size, unusual markings and voraciousness make it a formidable hunter.[1]

The tiger shark has distinctive dark black spots and vertical stripes/bars down its body resembling the pattern markings of a tiger, and although growing to considerable size, has impressive sudden bursts of speed when attacking prey, much like the land-based tiger. Male sharks grow to a max-

Figure 30: The Tiger Shark (© Shutterstock)

imum of four metres in length (estimated weight 400 kg - 600 kg), whilst females may grow to five metres or more, with the largest weighing from 900 to 1500 kilograms.

As a result of their bulkiness, the tiger shark appears to swim deceptively slowly. It uses its natural camouflage in the water to great advantage; it has the stealth of a tiger coupled with being one of the strongest swimmers in the shark family. This shark has other remarkable similarities to the 'big cats of the jungle'.

Its unique teeth are especially large, with very sharp and pronounced finely serrated edges for efficiently slicing through the flesh, bone and shells of hard-surfaced prey. It is a nocturnal hunter with large eyes and a sensitive layer at the back of those eyes for light detection, thus it is able to distinguish prey at night, even if hunting in murky water.

Unlike many other shark species, tiger sharks also have a protective membrane that covers the eyes during attacks to prevent possible inadvertent damage from the flailing prey. The tiger shark is usually a solitary hunter estimated to live up to 50 years[2] (the larger great white has an estimated lifespan of 70 years).[3] Jungle tigers may not live quite as long, but they certainly share an incredible number of common traits with this fierce marine prowler.

Great whites and tiger sharks were considered as sacred by the ancient Hawaiians, to be feared rather than honoured. Both species were provided with same name: *Niuhi* ('man-eating shark), and were evident in the local recorded mythology of Hawaii.[4] Both are considered to be the most dangerous and aggressive of sharks and accordingly, occupy the very top of the food chain around inshore waters.

If the tiger shark does have any peculiarity, it has to be a reputation for scavenging virtually anything encountered, particularly when food is scarce. It has the broadest diet of all sharks, and may even eat other smaller sharks. Inedible objects of human origin, particularly garbage or refuse – including tyres, vehicle licence plates and nails – may also be consumed if present in harbours, river inlets or other inshore areas.[5]

THE BARRACUDA

A much smaller saltwater fish that only grows up to two metres in length and weighs a maximum of 50 kilograms, but nonetheless just as ferocious as a shark and just as fearsome in appearance is the rather lethal great barracuda (*Sphyraena barracuda*).

This slender, streamlined, striped assassin has a large mouth/gape and a distinctive projecting lower jaw to accommodate all of its teeth. There is one closely set row of small razor-sharp, fang-like teeth along the outside of the jaw. Set within these teeth are a large dagger-like set that may prominently protrude out of its pointed snout. Long needle-like teeth are set in the opposing jaw.[6] These are ideal sets of teeth for ripping and chomping prey to pieces.

ON THE EDGE

Figure 31: The Beast Cometh (© Shutterstock)

It is the extreme acceleration of this fish that startles unsuspecting prey: it is estimated barracuda achieve maximum speeds of 50 to 60 kph in impressive short bursts. Barracuda take no prisoners and inflict tremendous destruction on other fish. They can also be difficult to catch, given their skill and agility in hunting.

Many years ago whilst residing in the remote West Kimberley coastal region of Western Australia, I managed to hook a very large barracuda on a fishing line with a shiny metallic lure being 'trolled' behind a boat. It was a monumental struggle trying to not only stop the beast from breaking my fragile line but actually catching it.

After several precarious minutes of intense struggle, the barracuda submissively approached the side of the boat, then simply rolled onto its side in order to gaze upon me, before ejecting the lure from its mouth and quietly swimming away. This hunter did not appreciate being the hunted.

Although as smaller fish and juveniles, barracuda hunt in huge schools of hundreds or thousands, upon maturity they become solitary predators. Try-

FEARSOME SWIMMERS

ing to stop a mature barracuda is like trying to stop 'the freight train of the seas'. This fish is truly 'the tiger of the sea'.

PIRANHAS

For a rather lightweight (3.5 kg) and appreciably smaller (14 -28 cm normal length) contender for the most predatory fish, is the South American black (redeye) piranha (*Serrasalmus rhombeus*). It is among the largest of the modern species (the red-bellied piranha – *Pygocentrus nattereri* – is larger, growing to a maximum length of 50 cm).

The black piranha's blade-like sharp teeth are tightly packed and interlocking in single rows, permitting rapid puncturing and shearing of prey. It has a bite with a maximum force of three times its bodyweight. Such strong jaws '... produce one of the most forceful bites measured in vertebrates'.[7]

Figure 32: The Small Fish with Powerful Jaws (© Shutterstock)

Piranha frequent freshwater rivers, reservoirs, lakes and floodplains rather than the high salt environment of oceans or seas, and possess a formidable reputation for voracious feeding.

However, piranha actually travel in shoals more for their own defensive protection from other predators than for hunting purposes. Nevertheless, a group of piranha could still launch quite a ferocious assault if sufficiently hungry.

Perhaps also not as well known is that they're actually omnivores, and their diet consists of fish (mainly), crustaceans, insects, worms, plants, fruits, seeds and other vegetation matter, as well as various vertebrates.[8] If food becomes scarce in their habitats, some have even been known to occasionally eat their own kind.

When devouring flesh other than fish, these omnivores usually only attack once the unfortunate animal is already deceased (carrion) or gravely injured. The teeth of this fish are similar in shape to a blade and are thus ideally adapted for meat-eating. Teeth are also replaced multiple times in the lifespan of the piranha, thus ensuring an efficient set of 'chompers'.[9]

The piranha is a primordial fish with fossil links to its earliest ancestors around 25 million years ago, although scientific studies suggest the modern species of piranha may have originated as recently as 1.8 million years ago[10] or as early as 9 million years ago.[11]

They have certainly been here for quite some time. However, despite the common perception of their ravenous feeding habits, these fish are foragers/scavengers who rarely exhibit hunting behaviour. They swim in large shoals (for safety in numbers) and are 'small fish with large, exceptionally sharp and specialised teeth', and not the dreaded hunters or ferocious predators of the waterways. However, they can still inflict serious injuries given the right circumstances.

THE MORAY EEL

The giant moray eel (*Gymnothorax javanicus*) is an enormous elongated fish, growing up to three metres in length (and occasionally over four metres), and weighing 30 kilograms.[12] Often mistaken for a gigantic snake, these marine eels have gills and are particularly elusive and solitary, inhabiting the shadowy crevices and other dark, narrow underwater coral/rock passages or gaps found in lagoons and near steep drop-offs to seaward tropical coral reefs.

They are carnivorous and can surprise their prey and unsuspecting divers by launching themselves out of concealed crevices without warning. They can also reverse far more readily than most fish, thus quickly retreating into the safety of their rocky lair.[13]

The most extreme feature of this eel is a rather unique 'double-jawed' attack. As they have poor suction compared to most fish, the moray eel first

Figure 33: Fangtooth Eels are not Sea Snakes (© Shutterstock)

grabs the prey with its sharp-toothed mouth before a second set of powerful jaws is pushed forward from the back of the throat to pull (swallow) the prey into the eel's throat.[14]

As with many marine predators, the moray eel has an impressive set of rear-facing teeth around the jaw making it extremely difficult for captured prey to escape, as well as extra teeth on the roof of the mouth to further assail their catch.

Some unfortunate divers who have inadvertently provoked these eels by venturing too close survive an eel attack but usually experience severe injury, particularly loss of fingers. The eel, with its poor eyesight, could easily mistake divers' hands and arms as potential prey.

SEA SNAKES

Sea snakes are air breathing reptiles with similarities to land-based snakes. The subtle adaptive changes that allow them to exist in a watery environment include a large lung capacity to enable them to stay underwater for up to two hours on a single breath. They have also evolved a flap to close across their nostrils when underwater, and their bodies are adapted to the marine environment, with a small head size and flattened tail to propel them quickly through water.[15] The marine species have paddle-like tails and laterally compressed bodies that almost resemble those of eels.

Sea snakes are capable of reaching a maximum depth of 100 metres and remaining submerged on the bottom to feed and rest, although many prefer shallow waters. Another interesting aspect of these unique reptiles is the sheer diversity of their skin colour patterns, ranging from boldly coloured banded varieties to the more subdued natural hues of camouflage commonly observed on land-based snakes.

These aquatic creatures are somewhat diminutive in size (up to a maximum length of two metres) when compared with the mythological gigantic 'seafaring serpents' reported by mariners – or imaginative sailors – in bygone centuries.

There are a vast array of 'water snakes' in the world, but only the Hydrophiidae 'family' completely inhabit marine environments for most or all their lives. Most species of sea snakes are potentially harmful for humans, with at least seven species thought to be capable of inflicting a fatal bite.

One of these is the beaked sea snake (*Enhydrina schistosa*). This snake's hooked nostril in front gives it a distinctive appearance of having a beak. It has been '…responsible for over half of sea snake bites and for almost 90 per cent of the fatalities resulting from them. The blue-belted sea snake (*Hydrophis cyanocinctus*) is the second most dangerous species and accounts for most of the remaining deaths'.[16]

The beaked sea snake's maximum dose of venom could kill 53 people. Of the land-based snakes, only the tiger snake (*Notechis scutatus*) is known to be capable of delivering a more deadly bite, although the taipan (*Oxyuranus scutella*) and the fierce snake (*Oxyuranus microlepidotus*) are suspected of being more dangerous.[17]

The beaked sea snake has also been described as 'cantankerous and savage', meaning that it is easily angered and becomes aggressive.[18]

This highly venomous snake is common in shallow open seas, near shore in shallow waters (coastal lagoons, harbours and bays) and estuaries, especially in the soft bottom (sand/mud) marine environments.[19] These are areas popular with people engaged in aquatic activities, particularly fishing and diving.

Most bites occur when people attempt to remove snakes from fishing/trawler nets and traps, or encounter them during sea dives. Fortunately, most sea snakes will attempt to escape when provoked or maltreated, though will still bite as a reaction if restrained or captured.

In stark contrast to the camouflaged sea snakes, the yellow-bellied sea snake (*Pelamis platurus*) or 'yellowbelly', which is the most widely distributed species of snake in the world, relies upon its unique bold contrasting colours and conspicuous markings to deter any potential predators.

With a bright yellow underside, a black back and combined markings on the tail, this relatively small (53-88 cm) pelagic snake clearly signals its poisonous nature, and may rarely need to resort to its potent venom as a defence.[20]

FESTIVALS AND OTHER EXTREMES

CLOWNS

'All the world's a stage,
And all the men and women merely players;
They have their exits and their entrances,
And one man in his time plays many parts ...'[1]
Shakespeare (1623)
– enter the Clown.

For the clown's role is many and varied, but above all else, it is to entertain and thereby provide pure enjoyment for people. By combining an unmistakable expressiveness and clever sense of humour with an exaggerated appearance, the clown is readily able to relate to human nature. Clowns portray a special form of emotional honesty in even the simplest performances.

Now imagine an enormous gathering of clowns in the one location, perhaps at a Clownfest or in a record-breaking parade. The outcome will always be the same – lots of floppy shoes, face paint, colourful elaborate apparel and organised chaos.

The annual Clown Costume Parade of *Cortejo de Fantasias de Palhaço* (Courting Clown Costumes) held in the quiet Portugese fishing village of Sesimbra is just such an example. It is also considered to be one of the largest clown congregations on the planet. Established in 1999 to introduce '… a little more color and animation to the town's rather sedate Monday afternoon Carnival parades…', it has grown progressively each year to '… some 4,000 fright-wigged, squeaky-nosed participants…' parading along the cobbled streets on the Monday of Carnival week.[2]

Figure 34: Sesimbra Clown Costume Parade (© CM Sesimbra)

The vibrantly colourful and lively festivity (clowns playing drums, tambourines and having fun) of the Sesimbra Carnival is further enhanced by the local residents who also dress as clowns '…to go about their day business…' and enjoy the parade of thousands of costumed clown revellers along the beachfront.[3] The company of so many masked clowns has to be an experience to be thoroughly enjoyed. Even the dogs are in costume.

FESTIVALS AND OTHER EXTREMES

The word 'clown' probably conjures many meanings to people, depending upon their perspective. Some may consider a clown to be a trickster, perhaps playing the fool, or simply an extroverted comical entertainer. Others might view clowns as terrifying and downright scary.[4] From my perspective, an 'extreme clown' is not someone who intends to frighten people, least of all children, but rather an accomplished entertainer or a dedicated part-time hobbyist committed to providing enjoyment to others.

The earliest origins of clowns were as *jesters* who provided amusing antics in the royal courts during the Middle Ages. By 'playing the fool', the jester was able to delight any audience. Jesters embellished their performances by wearing a cap and pointed shoes with bells that jingled as they moved.[5] Although those times are long past, clowns of the modern era perform at festivals, circuses, rodeos and on the stage, yet retain the same spirit for entertaining.

Figure 35: Clowning Around (© Shutterstock)

One of the most extreme elements to clowning is the individuality of the performers' appearances: 'each clown's costume and makeup are unique. In fact, one clown cannot wear his or her makeup in exactly the same way as any other clown.'[6] That includes any dogs as well. Clowns also have a worldwide organisation ('World Clown Association') that is open to jugglers, magicians and face painters as well, with a sensible clowning objective of bringing smiles and comic relief to others.

HOLI

Clowns are not the only ones who know how to enjoy themselves. The ancient Hindu religious 'Festival of Colours' known as *Holi* or *Rangwali Holi* is quite some celebration.

It is reputed to date back almost 1,500 years in India. Although traditionally convened in many countries with large Hindu populations, it has become popular with non-Hindus in many other parts of the world. In recent years, the festival has spread to parts of Europe and North America as a spring celebration of love, frolic and colours.[7] Recent festivals of colour have taken place in Barcelona (2014), Chelyabinsk, Russia (2015), Kiev, Ukraine and in Bulgaria (2017).

The renowned festival celebrates the seasonal ending of winter and start of spring, the religious triumph of inner good over evil and a spiritual thanksgiving, signified by a joyous free-for-all by revellers on the second day of overall festivities. The theme of this day is to play, laugh, forgive, give thanks and to heal oneself. The best way to start is to smear coloured powder and scented water on family, friends and random strangers.

This soon escalates into a raucous open air gathering where the participants cast dry powder ('gulal') of various bright colours upon fellow exuberant revellers. When mixed with water and sprayed on festival participants, it sticks like glue. Vast crowds pelt and smear each other without holding back:

'...where people smear each other with colours and drench each other. Water guns and water-filled balloons are also used to play and colour each other. Anyone and everyone is fair game, friend or stranger, rich or poor, man or woman, children and elders. The frolic and fight with colours occurs in the open streets, open parks, outside temples and buildings. Groups carry drums and other musical instruments, go from place to place, sing and dance. People visit family, friends and foes to throw coloured powders on each other, laugh and gossip, then share Holi delicacies, food and drinks'.[8]

Holi is truly a celebration of the heart and the mind. As one astute observer noted, it is '...as if everyone had passed under a rainbow waterfall or looked like a canvas of colours'.[9]

If seeking a hectic community festival of pure enjoyment and chaotic intermingling with lots of people, then be sure to bring along plentiful supplies of brightly coloured dry powder, coloured water, a water gun and plenty of motivation to be doused in powder, drenched in water or both. Participation is everything.

Figure 36: Festive Day of Vibrant Colours (© Shutterstock)

ON THE EDGE

UP HELLY AA

Shetland (also known as the Shetland Islands) is a relatively remote archipelago of about 100 islands located north-east of the island of Great Britain and comprises part of Scotland in the United Kingdom. It lies 170 kilometres from mainland Scotland and is a very sparsely populated region with only one town located at the port of Lerwick that is the capital of Shetland.[10]

This is a rugged coast set in a sub-Arctic region between the Atlantic Ocean and the North Sea, and in reasonable proximity to Scandinavia, and Norway in particular. As a result, the islands have an extensive heritage associated with the Vikings who colonised the region during the late 8th and 9th centuries.[11]

Given such a protracted history of Norse settlement (until the 15th century when it came under Scottish rule), it is not unusual that cultural links still remain today.

One Norse custom involves various fire festivals held throughout the islands' rural communities midway through the long exceptionally cold winters, with the largest '*Up Helly Aa*' festival convened in the capital Lerwick each year (regardless of howling gales, icy sleet and even snow at times). This midwinter festival marks the end of the Christmas and New Year celebratory season, with the most common interpretation of the '*Up Helly Aa*' expression appearing to be based on the Old Norse term *Helly* for holiday or weekend. Consequently, it could be translated as 'being the end of holidays'.[12]

The earliest origins of this celebratory festival initially involved squads of local young men dragging burning barrels of tar through the town on sleds to create mischief.[13] This was eventually replaced by much safer torch-lit processions in the late 19th century, as inspired by Nordic traditions.

In its modern form, the Lerwick *Up Helly Aa* fire festival celebrates the cultural ancestry of the islands with a distinctive spirit of camaraderie, geniality and revelry, combined with much singing, playing music and boisterous imbibing.

On the night of *Up Helly Aa* Day, a substantial procession of many hundreds carrying paraffin-soaked flaming torches is formed, with the lead group appropriately regaled in Viking armour and weapons, and remaining groups in colourful and diverse outfits.[14] The sheer spectacle of so many costumed participants bearing flame poles, and marching through the darkness to the sounds of band music is exceptionally stirring.

Upon reaching a replica Viking longship constructed for the festival, the participants in the procession encircle the empty vessel and, after completing the hearty song *Up Helly Aa*, they set the longship alight with their torches to create the ultimate bonfire. As the symbolic and sacrificial burning of the longship nears completion, it signals another Viking song from the gathering as a final requiem, aptly titled '*The Norseman's Home*'.[15]

Finally, the revelry switches to further celebratory functions and parties for the remainder of the night and on the following day as various groups visit many local halls and private residences. This has to be a thoroughly wondrous and enjoyable festival in the oldest traditions of comradeship and lighting one spectacular bonfire – Burn! Burn! Burn!

THE SURVA FESTIVAL

For another popular celebration with its origins in ancient and pagan traditions and rites, the Surva Festival ('The International Festival of Masquerade Games') convened annually in Bulgaria has to be on the extreme side of such gatherings. It is recognised as being one of the largest folklore festivals dedicated to ritualistic masks and disguises in the Balkans, and is held in the winter month of January in the industrial town of Pernik in the north-west of the country.

The choice of this town is particularly intriguing given its extensive history. The town's name of Pernik may have been derived from the name of the Slavic god of thunder and lightning, *Perun* (*–nik* is the Slavic placename suffix). However, given the thousand-year history of this settlement, and various sources from different times, there is no single explanation for the origin of its name.[16]

The thought of thunder and lightning certainly conjures quite some startling effects for me and by all accounts, so do the elaborate and sometimes grotesque costumed disguises, and uniquely vivid and sometimes scary masks. This is a celebratory festival to signify the end of the old year and welcome the upcoming spring season of plentiful harvest, prosperity and new life.

It is also about dispelling any 'evil spirits' that may potentially hinder this new beginning. To achieve this outcome, the ritualistic costumes and masks have to be realistic. All materials used are made from natural materials to retain the authenticity of the past. The elaborate rural suits to be worn are intricately made either of goat's hair, sheepskin and animal fur ('fur costumes), or from brightly coloured rags ('rag costumes').

These are embellished with beads, ribbons and poultry feathers wherever possible. The intention is to scare the spiritual monsters, and the loud noise of heavy metal bells worn around the waist provides further protection.

To complete the masquerade, various handmade masks add significant empowerment to the entire process and can be quite remarkable. The extreme masks may be adorned with horns, beaks, feathers or fur to represent the heads of peculiar creatures, or they may resemble weird and bizarre faces of beasts and be rather grotesque.

However, it is the symbolic 'dance of the masked men' that really entrances the spectacle. Inherent to the ritualistic celebration of dispelling evil spirits is the tightly co-ordinated and rhythmic steps of these groups, moving as one in complete unity. It certainly delivers a powerful message.

FESTIVALS AND OTHER EXTREMES

Figure 37: Masked People in Kukeri Dance to Scare Evil Spirits, The Surva Festival, Pernik, Bulgaria. Editorial credit: GEORGID/Shutterstock.com

FLOUR WARS

The small coastal fishing village of Galaxidi 200 kilometres west of the Greek capital Athens is home to a traditional ritualistic custom of *Alevromoutzouroma* or 'flour smudging/wars'. This community ritual goes back over 200 years and signifies the end of *Apokriatika* (Carnival) week on Clean Monday (also known as 'Pure Monday' or "Ash Monday') and the beginning of the 40-day Greek Orthodox Lent.[17]

The custom of flour smudging on the designated afternoon of this particular day involves thorough preparation to ensure the optimum outcome. Participants diligently prepare innumerable bags of dyed flour by adding various food colouring agents. They also paint their faces with charcoal (or ochre) to signify the townspeople faces apparently painted with ash when the ritual originally commenced. Old clothing is worn for very good reason:

'People wear rags, surgical masks and overalls with some keeping windbreaker hoods tightly clinched around their faces to ward off potentially severe cases of dry mouth.'[18]

Some revellers will even wear goggles, given the deluge about to be released on Clean Monday. After congregating in the town, where large quantities of the dyed flour are distributed in cloth bags, the participants march/parade to the nearby old harbour to commence the mayhem of 'flour wars'. In simplest terms, the ringing of cow bells signal the start of flour bombing, in which almost everyone (including onlookers standing too close) gets pelted and dusted from head to toe in coloured flour until supplies are exhausted.[19]

This is a considerable volume of flour, estimated around 1.5 tonnes or greater.[20]

For those that participate in the popular parade along the coastal road lining the harbour and the inevitable flour dusting, it is a chaotic and frenetic celebration of an ancient custom intent on providing great enjoyment, and quite a colourful appearance.

THE STAVELOT CARNIVAL

Wearing a mask allows people to adopt a different persona without fear of being identified. This is ideal when the mask being worn is hilarious, with a long, pronounced carrot-nose for added effect. *The Blancs Moussis* ('White Clad') characters of the Stavelot Carnival in Belgium wear such disguises. The costumes had their origins in makeshift disguises of white bedsheets and pillowcases.

These distinctly odd carnival characters, or immaculate White Monks, '… move through the crowds, grunting and laughing and hitting people with dried fish and [inflated] pigs' bladders … '.[21]

There is an interesting historical background to this tradition. Being cloaked in hooded and radiantly white, crisp sheets that shroud their very long and pointed carrot-noses and wearing strange masks is not necessarily weird, but more a parody of the merry-making Stavelot monks who regularly attended carnival festivities towards the end of the Middle Ages.[22]

The entertainment is really about the various antics of the *Blancs Moussis*: mimicking other people, showering spectators with copious quantities of confetti, dancing, grunting and jumping around a lot, as well as taunting people with pork bladders to join in the celebration. If this is not sufficient, 'confetti canons' dispense additional clouds of the coloured paper in a deluge onto spectators.[23]

This is a carnival of merriment and a celebration of frivolity and irreverence, ergo the 'grunting' or low indistinctive growling sounds instead of using speech.

Figure 38: *The Blancs Moussis* of Stavelot (© Shutterstock)

BOG SNORKELLING

Perhaps the Welsh Bog Snorkelling Championships held annually in the Waen Rhydd bog at Llanwrtyd Wells in the United Kingdom might offer more extreme personal entertainment?

This odd sporting event involves traversing a course (twice) along a flooded 55 metre long trench excavated through a peat bog. Participants must make their way through the mucky dark water without actually using conventional swimming strokes or surfacing (except for navigating). Writhing, kicking and splashing propulsion is permitted underwater, hence the snorkel, flippers and face mask.[24]

The fastest competitor becomes the current champion of this strange event, with success a matter of fractions of a second. The current world record holder in this particular peat bog is Kirsty Johnson (2014) who managed an incredible 1 minute 22.56 seconds of kicking, splashing and writhing through the aqua.[25]

Irishman Paddy Lambe set a new world record (2016) for bog snorkelling in Ireland of 1 minute 19 seconds.

Technique or lack of it appears to be everything when it comes to peat bogs. If propelling yourself underwater by thrashing and wiggling using 'flipper power' through an entanglement of weeds and decaying organic matter in cold discoloured water is for you, then why not bog snorkelling?

Wet and miserable weather to contribute further mud to the bog should not be a deterrent. Wearing bizarre swimming costumes is not recommended, unless attempting to win the novelty 'fancy dress' award.

FESTIVALS AND OTHER EXTREMES

RUBBER DUCKS

Missing and a reward offered for her capture – one gigantic inflatable yellow duck named Daphne last seen heading out to sea at a fair rate of knots, aided by a strong easterly wind.

It might not be a celebration of the weird or even some strange event, but Daphne the duck is definitely an extreme ducky. She was supposed to be the star attraction at an annual community ocean swim between jetties on the coast of Perth in Western Australia, but Daphne went missing, presumed swimming on prevailing ocean currents.[26]

Blame her escape on the prevailing wind but Daphne's handlers simply could not restrain the giant ducky adequately, and off she sailed out into the Indian Ocean. Smaller yellow duckies are accustomed to bath tubs with virtually no currents or extraneous breezes to aid their escape, but Daphne certainly seized her moment.

Somewhere out there is one gigantic inflatable yellow duck floating on the breeze and ocean currents. Bon voyage Daphne, and may you see the world without any collisions or deflation. We will miss you in Perth.

The following excerpt about another unlucky rubber duck entitled *Bad Luck Rubber Duck*, compiled by the contemporary English author of poems and limericks Mark Megson, captures the moment:

> 'A rubber ducky
> Was not so lucky
> He got flushed out to sea
> For many days
> On the ocean waves
> Would that rubber ducky be
>
> He sailed through sun
> He sailed through storm
> To places cold and places warm …

> ... It's not so bad
> The luck he had
> As now the duck is free
>
> Because he sails in the biggest bath of all
> When the tide takes him out to sea.' [27]

The world's largest yellow inflatable ducky is the *Rubber Duck* designed by Dutch artist Florentijan Hofman as a gigantic 'floating art piece'. Since 2007 it has visited many major cities and towns across the world in various design sizes. The waterfowl's maximum sculptured size was its original version of 32 metres in height, 26 metres in width and 20 metres in length.[28]

It is usually transported by tug boat or barge, and so has only minimal opportunity to break free from its benign existence of floating around the various harbours, lakes, rivers and other waterways of the world over the past ten years.

A large fleet of much smaller buoyant rubber ducks was lost overboard from a container ship during a storm in the Pacific Ocean en route from Hong Kong and the west coast of USA in January 1992.

These little characters have '... gone on wandering the oceans of the world ever since, like a doomed plastic-feathered flock of ancient mariners'.[29] The number of Floatee polyethylene bath toys that were released from a single sea-container was 28,800, including 7,200 yellow ducklings.[30]

NEON TECHNODREAMS

What is the special decorative appeal of glowing luminous neon lighting when used to illustrate words or pictures in advertising or commercial signage and on combined signscapes? After all, 'In its natural state, Neon gas is unremarkable, without colour or smell and something for the chemist …'[1]

However, rarefied [low pressure] neon or today's different combinations of gases and chemical fluorescent coatings confined in long sealed gas-discharge tubes and energised with high voltage create a distinctively brilliant colours. For example, hydrogen gas produces red, mercury produces blue and carbon dioxide yields white.

Pure neon gas only produces about one third of all colours, mostly various shades of red, orange and intense pink. The majority of colours (shades of yellow, green, blue, violet, softer pink and white) are produced in "neon tubes" by using argon, which is another inert gas.

By sequential programming of these colourful emissions, the resultant dynamic light patterns produce animated images – a perception of movement to the human eye.

Figure 39: The Flying Bird (© Shutterstock)

It is the artistic design and intricate fabrication of the multicolour luminous tubing into curvilinear recognisable shapes that produces such spectacular outcomes. One such highly visual neon sign of the myriad emerging in the early 1950s was in Las Vegas, Nevada in the USA: 'On the Stardust [Casino] a plastic planet shone, with neon tubes and light bulbs creating a cloud of stars and shooting starlight up into make-believe space.'[2]

Another dazzling historical example, also from Las Vegas, and erected in 1951, was Vegas Vic; a 12 metre neon cowboy sign with a friendly, welcoming appearance, and the ability to move arms, wink an eye, hold a cigarette and blow smoke rings.[3]

The application of neon signage has traditionally been most successful in providing eye-catching graphics for commercial premises, such as bars, restaurants and recreational outlets, as well as to promote a saleable product, from soft drink and beer to tyres and photocopiers.

The vibrant cool colours and exciting electric designs promote an attractive image to the beholder. Many major cities of the world such as New York, Paris, Hong Kong and Tokyo have embraced this neon empire.

Figure 40: Eye-Catching Graphics (© Shutterstock)

Although this popularity has waned in some applications with the advent of new technologies, such as fluorescent signage and more recently LEDs (light-emitting diodes), proponents of neon technology maintain it still has significant advantages over LEDs, including an extensive colour palette and a creatively flexible system of illumination.[4]

For high quality neon illumination, where better to start than the classic 1982 futuristic science fiction movie *Blade Runner* set in the year 2019.

'… the grand commercial projects … are displayed on gigantic overhead screens … The old-style neon advertisements symbolize an imperfect, authentic urban life that has survived despite genetic manipulation and colonization of the universe'.[5]

The neon art frequently displayed in the background throughout this movie provides an inspiring sense of the old-fashioned technology from the 20th century still retained in the culture of the next century. The fusion of vivid and often stark neon lights on streets, in arcades or on buildings provides subtle glamour to a story about future advancing technologies.

To gauge the extremes of artistic neon illumination, the visionary endeavours of contemporary sculptors perhaps represent the best choice to examine this magical medium of the neon-tube – the magicians of light playing with mystery:

> 'Neon light is the future, the excitement, and the dynamics of inter-stellar society.'[6] Jon Miskinis (1970)

> 'Neon is fire, or something which approximates it, a flame that consumes or illuminates.'[7] Vincente A. Pineda

> 'I love neon — the fantastic world created by light and glass. The light suddenly appearing in clear glass, going through it, reflecting and curving its way through the tubing, composing as it does beautiful colors and shapes …'[8] Nobuyuki Sasaki (1988)

> 'Electro man is the result of my desire to create my own Frankenstein. He's 120 feet of red neon and approximately ten beer signs of brightness. He's dangerous, he sizzles and hums, and he is extremely difficult to look at.'[9] Michael Fury (1986)

When the badly insulated cabling of neon lighting equipment is subjected to rainfall in the right circumstances, such as in tropical humidity, it can make a buzzing sound like insects ('neon music'),[10] but really neon signage is about visual perception ('the neon glow') rather than music. For an appreciation of the 'language of neon', a short poem by American writer Searich (2012) entitled *Neon Light* would impress:

'Mystery of night,
Reflecting,
Street scenes,
With ghosts of,
Neon Light,
Blinking red,
Dark blue night hues,
A mesmerizing stare.[11]

Perhaps what truly makes the neon glow so important to many of us is its originality; people can have personal designs or their names configured in spectacular neon on their own sign. Neon really does make us glow.

GLOW PARTIES

Neon signs are not the only artistic symbol to glow. People decorated in fluorescent paint also 'glow' when exposed in a dark environment to the long-wave ultraviolet ('UV') frequencies of light, such as from an ultraviolet 'blacklight' lamp.[12]

Such lamps generate ultraviolet light that is invisible to the naked eye while filtering out as much visible light as possible.[13] The paint is luminous and gives off visible light by 'fluorescence 'as an unusual glow, producing elaborate visual effects on participants' faces and bodies.

What transpires when you have a gathering of like-minded glow people intent upon enjoying themselves is an event broadly described as a *fluoro or glow party*. The essential addition of 'black light cannons' is a prerequisite for such festivities – it projects the necessary special UV wavelength for absorption by the fluoro makeup, so everyone glitters.

UV blacklight/glow parties around the world have been electric when further enhanced by stunning masquerade outfits, reflective mirror balls, extensive glow sticks, dazzling strobe lights and 'effect' laser lights that gen-

ON THE EDGE

Figure 41: Let the Party Begin (© Shutterstock)

erate vibrant narrow shafts of glow at random, and the essential ingredient of suitably honed musical vibes.

Tomorrowland – which began in 2005 – located south of Antwerp in Belgium is possibly one of the world's largest, and most notable music festivals based upon popularity,[14] offering an immense plethora of electronic dance music and almost overwhelming nightly light shows and stunning visuals. The annual festivals remain so popular that demand exceeds supply for entry tickets each year, with a resultant extensive wait list.

However, for an even greater visual feast, the Ultra Music Festival held in Miami, USA since 1999 certainly continues to contribute outstanding kaleidoscopes of colour and patterns across several stages – a form of visual artistry for the masses.

FOOTBRIDGES AND GNOMES

Bridges are structures made of wood, concrete, stone, brick or metal that span streams, rivers, ravines and other previously inaccessible strategic geographical passages. They link and unify communities, cities and countries. They are designed with the primary purpose of enabling travellers, transportation elements (such as roads and railways) and service utilities to pass from one side to the other, thus bypassing the underlying obstacle(s).

For a variety of reasons in more remote areas of the world, they may be constructed by necessity from the most readily available local materials, such as timber. In these areas, they may be configured to address the challenges of the harsh terrain or turbulent water bodies being traversed. Turbulent water courses and limited available access can mean a footbridge (rather than a bridge capable of carrying vehicles) is the only way of crossing the river.

Contemporary Turkish playwright and novelist Mehmat Murat Ildan's wise

ON THE EDGE

Figure 42: Wooden Footbridge (© Shutterstock)

words convey quite a message in this respect: 'The wisdom of the bridge comes from the fact that it knows the both sides, it knows the both shores!'[1] (*Mehmet Murat ildan*, 2013)

'The fate of the bridges is to be lonely; because bridges are to cross not to stay!'[2] (*Mehmet Murat ildan*, 2011). I certainly concur with his sentiment not to linger, on this footbridge in particular.

Timber is a very useful medium for pedestrian footbridges, especially when fabricated as planks. However, when the local supply does not quite suffice to complete the repair of such a footbridge, it may take on a rather daunting appearance to the casual observer.

If American poet and educator Henry Wadsworth Longfellow had possibly been that casual observer, perhaps the following excerpts from his 1845 poem *The Bridge* may have signalled his thoughts about such a footbridge:

FOOTBRIDGES AND GNOMES

Figure 43: Broken Footbridge (© Shutterstock)

I stood on the bridge at midnight, …

… Among the long, black rafters
The wavering shadows lay,
And the current that came from the ocean
Seemed to lift and bear them away;

As, sweeping and eddying through them,
Rose the belated tide, …

… And like those waters rushing
Among the wooden piers,
A flood of thoughts came o'er [over] me
That filled my eyes with tears …'[3]

These footbridges are probably not as daunting as the world's longest pedestrian/walker suspension bridge, which opened in July 2017 in Switzerland. The 494 metre bridge spans the deepest cut valley in the country and is located 85 metres above the ground at its highest point.

At only 65 centimetres wide (0.65 metres), and with a grated metal floor, it provides quite a view below for the intrepid traveller. Best described as most suitable '… For hikers with no fear of heights', and with the '… warning about crossing the bridge during a storm, due to "danger of lightning"…'[4]

GNOMES

So what do gnomes have in common with footbridges? To the casual observer, it would seem there is no common link, apart from one minor detail. Gnomes are relatively tiny creatures and barely detectable to humans, preferring to keep well out of sight wherever possible. Just imagine how many steps a gnome would need to take to cross a footbridge almost 500 metres long. Not that we would ever see one eventually crossing a footbridge, given their ability to remain almost invisible.

Apparently they are quite adept at hiding in the shadows under bushes or remaining in hidden corners above and below ground.[5] As one description of their origins found in folk tradition specifies:

> '… gnomes were supposed to live underground [earth-dwellers], moving through earth as freely as if it were air, & their function was supposed to be to guard the treasures of the earth [mine spirits].'[6]

A gnome or diminutive humanoid being is thought to be both imaginary and mystical, ageless and legendary, borne of folklore origins and children's fairy stories. They are described across many ancient cultures and have come to be recognised in modern times by the small ornamental replicas that decorate gardens, lawns and village parks.

FOOTBRIDGES AND GNOMES

Of course such garden gnomes may come in all shapes and sizes, but the 'classic' garden variety is typically an aged bearded man wearing a pointed cap.

To understand more about gnomes, one has to appreciate the importance of their caps:

> 'A gnome without a cap is not a gnome … Rather, it [the cap] is an indispensable head covering, protection against such unsuspected blows from above as are dwelt by falling twigs, acorns, or hailstones, and against attacks by animals or birds … The gnome reveals his individuality as much with his cap as with the shape of his nose…'[7]

The gnome is also reputed to know '… exactly what the weather will be long in advance … still goes about in rain, hail, mist, heat and cold – weather, after all does not make much difference to him'. For example, 'In thunderstorms, the gnome is in little danger of being struck by lightning because he is so small.' However, 'The only danger that may befall gnomes in winter, especially in hilly terrain, is that if they are out walking they may get rolled up in a natural snowball as it tumbles down.'[8]

Many people love to collect gnomes and display them accordingly in the outdoor environment, not only to enhance the appearance of their gardens and lawns, but also to populate vegetated areas thus providing some quirky/eccentric results. British philosopher, political economist and civil servant John Stuart Mill's quotation on eccentricity (1859) provides some guidance:

> '…the amount of eccentricity in a society has generally been proportional to the amount of genius, mental vigour and moral courage which it contained'.[9]

So just how many gnomes can one accumulate? The official world record as of 2015 stands at 2,042 gnomes and pixies on a 1.6 hectare (4 acres) Gnome Reserve in West Putford, North Devon in England.[10] Now that is quite a group of gnomes.

ON THE EDGE

Figure 44: Collection of Hand Decorated and Painted Garden Gnomes, Canberra Annual Flower Show, ACT 2008

Editorial credit: Steve Lovegrove/Shutterstock.com

However, a significantly larger population of these ornamental characters has yet to be officially listed: this collection is located at the aptly named 'Gnomesville' in bushland of the Ferguson Valley in the South-West region of Western Australia. It is a mystery how the immense community, estimated to contain more than 10,000 garden gnomes in an area of approximately one half hectares, first appeared in this rural setting in 1995. Even more mystifying is the fact that their numbers are continuously growing.

Several opinions abound as to their origin, including the placement of a solitary gnome '... leaning on a shovel, watching road workers as they constructed a roundabout in the middle of nowhere following a school bus accident in the then y-intersection ...'[11] Further gnomes were subsequently added, and the completed roundabout became the gnome's oval: '... locals put some football posts in and painted them in a football guernsey. Every night new spectators would come and the scores would change'.[12]

Another version of the story is that visitors added their own gnomes beside the roundabout so that the original gnome would no longer be lonely. As the tradition continued and the community grew extensively, the local shire eventually relocated them to a small tract of land adjacent to roadside. Such was the 'organic' growth over the years that Gnomesville was rated in 2014 by the AMEX online magazine *Departures* as the third best road trip stop in Australia.[13, 14]

What is so impressive about such an enormous and random gathering of gnomes from all parts of the world is that they occupy almost every conceivable space. They are in the trees, on logs, paths and fences, found in various groups or simply perched alone. Many are engaged in activities, from flying planes, playing sports and fishing to family gatherings. Every gnome has a place in this outdoor setting.

> 'Year after year, more gnomes appear on foot or by car. Though everyone knows, a gnome likes to roam, a gnome needs a home – AND GNOMESVILLE IS THE BEST HOME BY FAR!!!'[15]

Perhaps the incredible popularity of garden gnomes worldwide has to do with ancestral beginnings in rural areas where they were regarded as good luck charms for growing of crops and raising livestock. Whatever the reasons, gnomes have been around centuries: 'The world's oldest garden gnome, called Lampy, has been living at Lamport Hall in the UK for 125 years …'[16] This is quite an extended existence for a gnome, given an apparent preference to remain out of sight of people.

OVER THE EDGE

Fly like a bird,
Swim like a fish,
Dance like a leaf on the breeze,
Walk in the pouring rain
or simply wear the mask of a clown.

Fly with paper wings,
Skate on thin ice,
Ride the whirlwind,
Reach the precipice,
Live for the moment.

Whatever it takes to experience extreme life,
However exhilarating may be the world's natural wonders,
Life can be incredibly brief and fraught with peril.

The challenge lies in surviving the journey.

OVER THE EDGE

Figure 45: Surviving the Journey (© Shutterstock)

For every action there are always consequences. The solution is to choose the right consequences and still enjoy the moment. The exhilaration of floating freely through the atmosphere, riding the ocean's waves or traversing snowfalls/sheet ice, hiking treacherous mountainous terrain, safely crossing a rickety footbridge high above a raging river, or surviving the challenge of nature's most severe elements; all require personal courage and committed endeavour. Exotic animals, birds and marine life also live on the edge in their daily lives, but have mostly adapted over time to survive, often despite many constraints.

So what does it really mean to go 'over the edge'? American journalist and author Hunter Stockton Thompson suggested one possibility in 1966, as follows:

> '... The Edge ... There is no honest way to explain it because the only people who really know where it is are the ones who have

> gone over.
>
> The others -- the living -- are those who pushed their control as far as they felt they could handle it, and then pulled back, or slowed down, or did whatever they had to when it came time to choose between Now and Later …'[1]

Such dire consequences seem astutely captured in the following partial quotation of the 2012 poem *Not for Me a Youngman's Death* by English poet, broadcaster, children's author and playwright Roger McGough:

> "Not for me a youngman's death
> Not a car crash, whiplash …
>
> … Not a horse-riding paragliding
> mountain climbing fall, death.
> Motorcycle into an old stone wall
> you know the kind of death, death
>
> *My nights are rarely unruly.*
> *My days of all-night parties*
> *are over, well and truly…*
>
> … Let me die an oldman's death …
> Not … 'What a waste of life' death.'[2]

This is definitely the sombre side to extreme life, but there is also an upside to simply having fun and making the most of one's endeavours – after all, life is one continuous adventure after another. Celebratory festivals, collecting gnomes, diving into massive ball pits, appreciating exotic wildlife and dynamic artistic neon signage are but a few examples of less strenuous participation.

> 'It is only when we truly know and understand that we have a limited time on earth and that we have no way of knowing when our time is up that we will begin to live each day to the fullest, as if it were the only one we had.'[3] St Augustine (354-430 AD)

For a final appreciation of being 'over the edge', the following words by contemporary American author M.H. Boroson may be most salient: 'Nothing is ever as simple as it seems. At the edge of perception, weird things dance and howl.'[4]

REFERENCES

CHAPTER 1: On The Edge

1. Strode, Muriel, 'Wind-Wafted Wild Flowers', in *The Open Court: Devoted to the Science of Religion, the, Religion of Science, and the Extension of the Religious Parliament Idea,* vol.17, no.8, Section: Miscellaneous, August 1903, p.505.

2. Raymo, C., 'The Bird And The Fish', in *The Soul of the Night – An Astronomical Pilgrimage*, 1985, p.205.

CHAPTER 2: Free Fall

1. Quick, D., New Atlas, 27 October 2014, Remarkable People - Google exec sets new high-altitude skydiving world record, https://newatlas.com/alan-eustace-world-record-skydive-stratex/34423/. Accessed 15 January 2018.

2. Waring, R. (ed.), *Extreme Skydiving*, National Geographic, 2010, p.4.

REFERENCES

3. ibid., pp.18-22.

4. Fédération Aéronautique Internationale Website, Parachuting Sports, https://www.fai.org/sport/parachuting?f[0]=fai_event_year%3A2018. Retrieved 15 January 2018.

5. Wikipedia Encyclopedia, Wingsuit Flying, January 2018, https://en.wikipedia.org/wiki/Wingsuit_flying. Retrieved 16 January 2018.

6. Guinness World Records, Longest (duration) wingsuit flight, 20 April 2012, http://www.guinnessworldrecords.com/world-records/longest-(duration)-wingsuit-flight.

7. ibid., Greatest horizontal distance flown in a wingsuit, 30 May 2016.

8. Wikipedia Encyclopedia, Wingsuit BASE jump records:Longest, https://en.wikipedia.org/wiki/Wingsuit_flying. Retrieved 16 January 2018.

9. Waring, op.cit., 'Mark Calland' on Speed Skydiving, p.7.

10. Lawson, J., 'Dean Potter is the Man That Can Fly', in *Climb* ZA – *Everything Climbing*, 13 February 2012, http://www.climbing.co.za/2012/02/dean-potter-is-the-man-who-can-fly/. Retrieved 16 January 2018.

11. BBC Television, 'The People of Paradise: Episode 1 of 6', in *The Land Divers of Pentecost*, First Broadcast 21 April 1960. Retrieved 2 February 2018.

12. BBC News, "*World's 'first' bungee jump in Bristol captured on film*", 10 November 2014. http://www.bbc.com/news/av/uk-england-29819029/world-s-first-bungee-jump-in-bristol-captured-on-film. Retrieved 2 February 2018.

13. Sagert, K.B., *Encyclopedia of Extreme Sport*, 2009, pp.26-7.

CHAPTER 3: Up and Away

1. Samuel, E., 'If Only I Could Fly', *Poetry Soup*, 2015, https://www.poetrysoup.com/poems/best/hot-air_balloon. Retrieved 30 January 2018.

2. Hicks, K., *Hot Air Ballooning*, 2013, pp.18-19.

3. Wikipedia Encyclopedia, 'Accidents and incidents', in *Hot air balloon*, January 2018, https://en.wikipedia.org/wiki/Hot_air_balloon#Accidents_and_incidents. Retrieved 22 January 2018.

4. Hewitt, A., '10 Biggest Hot Air Balloon Festivals in the World', 1 February 2017, https://www.insidermonkey.com/blog/10-biggest-hot-air-balloon-festivals-in-the-world-527022/?singlepage=1. Retrieved 30 January 2018.

5. Bristol International Balloon Fiesta 2018. http://www.bristolballoonfiesta.co.uk/ Accessed 30 January 2018.

6. Hicks, op.cit., p.22.

7. Samuels, G., 'Russian priest breaks round-the-world ballooning record', in *The Independent Newspaper*, 24 July 2016, http://www.independent.co.uk/news/world/australasia/russian-priest-fedor-konyukhov-round-the-world-hot-air-helium-balloon-record-a7153356.html.

8. ibid., Samuels, 2016.

9. Kotar, A.L and Gessler J.E. (ed.), Preface, *in Ballooning: A History, 1792-1900*, 2014, p.1.

10. ibid., p.4.

11. Sahni,P, 'Hang Gliding vs Paragliding', Mountaineering.asia, 15 February 2016, https://mountaineering.asia/hang-gliding-vs-paragliding/. Accessed 1 February 2018.

12. World Air Sports Federation (FAI) 'Hang Gliding and Paragliding', in *Records* , ID 16577, p.27, https://www.fai.org/records. Retrieved 1 February 2018.

13. Roberts, G., Ward, J., and White, J., 'A Record Hang Gliding Ride on the Texas Wind', in *The New York Times: Sports Section*, Issue 1 November 2013, Retrieved 1 February 2018.

14. Hurni, M., 'Jon Durand Hang Gliding World Record Attempt 2016', *Hang Gliding*, 27 July 2016, https://www.redbull.com/au-en/jonny-durand-hang-gliding-world-record-attempt, Retrieved 2 February 2018.

REFERENCES

15. Sagert, op.cit.,'Hang Gliding', p.75.

16. Dougherty,S., 'Across the Country', in *Hang Gliding and Paragliding Association of Canada National Newsletter*, Vol.8,Issue 4, December 1994, p.21.

17. World Air Sports Federation (FAI), 'Judy Leden multiple champion and record holder', in *News –Personalities*, http://old.fai.org/news/personalities/35338-judyleden, Retrieved 2 February 2018.

18. Sagert, op.cit., p.74.

19. McElrah, Hugh, Capital Hang Gliding and Paragliding Association, In 'Flights of Fancy: Hang Gliding Called the "Purest" Way to Fly' Article, *Washington Times*, Issue 20 June 2005.

20. Dvorsky, G., 'The world's largest ball pit has a whopping one million balls in it', 1 November 2013, www.io9.gizmodo.com. Retrieved 2 February 2018.

21. Guinness World Records, 'Largest Ball Bath/Pit/Pool', 25 September 2015, http://www.guinnessworldrecords.com/world-records/largest-ball-bath-pit-pool.

22. Hawke, S., ABC News, 'Sydney Festival: Plastic balls, synthetic sand used to create event's signature beach', 7 January 2017, http://www.abc.net.au/news/2017-01-06/sydney-fetival-2017-plastic-balls-safe-beach/8166044. Accessed 2 February 2018.

CHAPTER 4: Air and Water

1. Labrecque, E., *Cliff Diving*, 2012, p.29.

2. Guinness World Records' Title, Archived 3 December 2015, http://www.guinnessworldrecords.com/news/2015/12/new-photos-laso-schaller-completes-the-highest-cliff-jump-ever-attempted-408930. Retrieved 23 January 2018.

3. World High Diving Federation, General Regulations - October 2017, https://www.whdf.com/information/general-regulations/. Retrieved 23 January 2018.

4. Wikipedia Encyclopedia, La Quebrada Cliff Divers, Archived 7 July 2017, https://en.wikipedia.org/wiki/La_Quebrada_Cliff_Divers. Retrieved 25 January 2018.

5. Stanford, B., The Savage History of Cliff Jumping, Archived 19 November 2015, bigswings.blogspot.com.au/2015/11/the-savage-history-of-cliff-diving-by. Retrieved 25 January 2018.

6. Cliff Diving Daredevils Take on the Sport of Kings and Warriors, Archived 8 November 2009, http://abcnews.go.com/GMA/Weekend/highs-lows-cliff-diving/story?id=9024936. Accessed 4 February 2018.

7. Labrecque, op.cit., p.6.

8. Red Bull Cliff Diving, History in the making – Celebrating 50 stops of Red Bull Cliff Diving, 8 October 2015, http://cliffdiving.redbull.com/en_BA/article/history-making.

9. Macmillan Dictionary, Buzz Word 'tombstoning', https://www.macmillandictionary.com/buzzword/entries/tombstoning.html.

10. Wordnik - Wiktionary, 'tombstoning', https://www.wordnik.com/words/tombstoning.

11. Maxwell, K., 'Tombstoning' in *Brave New Words: A Language Lover's Guide to the 21st Century*, 2006.

12. Hapgood, A., 'The Backstory', in *Kiteboarding: Where it's at...*, 2014, p.8.

13. KiteNews.fr, Christophe Salvaing, Archived 13 November 2017, http://www.kitenews.fr/nouveau-record-monde-5797-noeuds-soit-10736-kmh/. Retrieved 26 January 2018.

14. PKR Kiteboarding, News - Nick Jacobsen: Kite World Record for Biggest Jump on WOO, 28.6 Metres, Archived 21 February 2017, https://pkrkiteboarding.com/nick-jacobsen-kite-world-record-biggest-jump-woo-28-6-mt/. Accessed 26 January 2018.

15. Jones, L., 'Another new world record for kite surfing set by Louis Trapper', *Xtreme Sport*, Archived 21 September 2010, xtremesport4u.com/extreme-sports-personalities/another-new-record-for-kite-surfing/.

REFERENCES

Accessed 29 January 2018.

16. Wikipedia Encyclopedia, 'Wakestyle', in *Kiteboarding -Terminology and Jargon*, https://en.wikipedia.org/wiki/Kiteboarding. Retrieved 24 January 2018.

CHAPTER 5: Extreme Water Pursuits

1. Guinness World Records, Published 9 May 2012. "78-foot wave surfed by Garrett McNamara confirmed as largest ever ridden". Retrieved 17 January 2018.

2. Wikipedia Encyclopedia, Garrett McNamara, World Record, January 2013, https://en.wikipedia.org/wiki/Garrett_McNamara.

3. Council on Tall Buildings and Urban Habitat (CTBUH), Height Calculator, 'Office Building Category', http://www.ctbuh.org/HighRiseInfo/TallestDatabase/Criteria/HeightCalculator.

4. Marcus, B., 'Size Matters' quote by Buzzy Trent, in *Extreme Surf*, 2008, p.146.

5. ibid., p.114.

6. International Canoe Federation (ICF), Canoeing, Kayaking and Rowing: So what's the difference anyway? in *Planet Canoe*, Archived from the original on 15 August 2012, Canoeicf.com.

7. Wikipedia Encyclopedia, 'Creeking', in *Whitewater Kayaking*, https://en.wikipedia.org/wiki/Whitewater_kayaking. Retrieved 19 January 2018.

8. Garcia, E., Matador Network, Paddling – *Kayaking some of the best whitewater on Earth: Fjord Norway*, 28 October 2013, https://matador-network.com/sports/kayaking-some-of-the-best-whitewater-on-earth-fjord-norway.

9. Whiting, K., and Varette, K., 'Running Waterfalls', in *Whitewater Kayaking: The Ultimate Guide*, 2nd Ed., 2012, p.150.

10. ibid., p.103.

11. Heller, P. 'Preface', in *Hell Or High Water: Surviving Tibet's Tsongpo River*, 2014.

12. Yeung, Y. and Shen, J., (eds.), 'Tibet', in *Developing China's West: A Critical Path to Balanced National Development*, 2004, p.553.

13. Encyclopædia Britannica (eds.), Apurímac River, Peru, 1999/2011, https://www.britannica.com/place/Apurimac-River. Accessed 22 January 2018.

14. Whiting and Varette, op.cit., p.204, 262.

15. AIDA International (International Association for Development of Apnea), "World Records". Archived from the original on 17 August 2016. Retrieved 22 January 2018.

16. Nestor, J., *Deep: Freediving, Renegade Science, and What The Ocean Tells Us About Ourselves*, 2014, pp.9-10.

17. ibid., p.8.

CHAPTER 6: Snow and Ice

1. Wikipedia Encyclopedia, Tour Skating, 5 October 2017, https://en.wikipedia.org/wiki/Tour_skating. Retrieved 7 February 2018.

2. Heathcote, J.M., and Tebbutt, C.G., 'The Origin and Development of Skating', in *Skating*, 1892, p.6.

3. Flood, B., and Papenhausen, R. (ed.), 'St.John's early sporting history', in *Saint John: A Sporting Tradition 1785-1985, 1985*, p.27.

4. Harris, M., Ice skating tours on natural ice in Sweden (2006), Updated 1 July 2015, http://frozentime.se/skating/skating.html. Accessed 8 February 2018.

5. Seura, S. K. and Bosley, K. (translator and editor), 'Otto Manninen', in *Skating on the Sea: Poetry from Finland*, 1997, p.161.

6. Hill, D., *Snowboarding: The Fundamentals And Beyond*, 2001, p.3.

7. ibid., pp.15-17.

8. Roberts, W.O. and Bull, R.C., 'Medical', in *Bull's Handbook of Sports Injuries*, 2nd Ed., 2004, p.550.

9. ibid., p.555.

REFERENCES

10. Howard, A., 'Watch Jamie Barrow break the world snowboard speed record', in *Travel/Ski News*, The Telegraph, 20 April 2016, http://www.telegraph.co.uk/travel/ski/news/jamie-barrow-breaks-british-and-world-snowboard-speed-records/. Retrieved 14 February 2018.

11. Horton, J., Higher, faster, longer! Snowboarding world records, Red Bull: Snowboarding, 14 August 2015, https://www.redbull.com/au-en/overview-of-world-records-in-snowboarding. Retrieved 14 February 2018.

12. Hill, op.cit.,'The History of Snowboarding', p.1.

CHAPTER 7: The Surging Aqua

1. Nalivkin, D.V., 'Waterspouts', in *Hurricanes, storms and tornadoes: Geographic characteristics and geological activity*, 1983, p.319.

2. Gordon, A.H. 'Waterspouts', Part 1,2, *The Marine Observer*, vol.21, 1951, pp.47-60.

3. Nalivkin, op.cit., p.320.

4. Szilagyi, W., 'The Great Waterspout Outbreak of 2003', in *CMOS Bulletin SCMO*, vol.31, No.6, December 2003, p.160.

5. Tornadoes: Waterspouts, in *The Gallery of Natural Phenomena: the earth, the sea, the sky –and beyond*, 2010, http://www.phenomena.org.uk/tornadoes/page6/page6.html. Accessed 19 February 2018.

6. Popov, N.I., *The waterspouts near the shores of the Black Sea*, Meteorological Instituta, Gidrol., no.5, 1955, p.35.

7. Momtastic WebEcoist , 'Maelstrom of Saltstraumen', in *Nature and Ecosystems:10 Magnificent Maelstroms*, http://www.momtastic.com/webecoist/2009/07/24/10-magnificent-maelstroms-and-destructive-whirlpools/. Retrieved 19 February 2018.

8. Extreme Marine, 'Formation:In the Straight and Narrow', in *Whirlpools: Extreme Eddies or Magnificent Maelstroms*, 1 December 2016, http://extrememarine.org.uk/2016/12/whirlpools-extreme-eddies-or-magnificent-maelstroms/. Accessed 19 February 2018.

9. Poe, E.A., 'A Descent into the Maelstrom', in *Graham's Magazine*, No. CLXXXV, Israel Post, New York, May 1841.

10. Howell, S., and Saxena, S (ed.), *Whirlpools*, 2017, p.23.

11. ibid., p.4.

12. 'The Buccaneer Archipelago – West Part Section 3.71, Northwest Coast of Australia – Cape Londonerry to Cape Leveque', in *Sailing Directions (Enroute) North, West, and South Coasts of Australia*, Publication 175, 12th Ed., 2014, p.72.

13. Zell, L.,'Talbot Bay to Pender Bay', in Wild Discovery Guides - Kimberley Coast: *A guide to the Kimberley Coast wilderness: north-western Western Australia*, 2nd Ed., 2007, p.113.

14. 'Passages in Sunday Strait Section 3.93, Northwest Coast of Australia – Cape Londonerry to Cape Leveque', in *Sailing Directions (Enroute) North, West, and South Coasts of Australia*, Publication 175, 12th Ed., 2014, p.77.

15. ibid., p.77

16. Scott, A.W. (Sandy), 'Whirlpool Straits', in *A Traveller's Guide: Kimberley Coast: Bays, Basins, Islands and Estuaries*, 2012, pp.77-8.

17. Read, I.G., 'Tides', in *Continent of Extremes: Recording Australia's Natural Phenomena*, 1998, pp.84-5.

18. NASA Earth Observatory, *High and Low Tides in Bay of Fundy*, 14 June 2016, https://earthobservatory.nasa.gov/IOTD/view.php?id=6650. Retrieved 20 February 2018.

19. Garrow, S. C., *Big tide country: a book about the Kimberley's tides and tidal life*, 2002, pp.11-13.

20. ibid., p.13.

21. Zell, op.cit., 'Kimberley Coast', p.114.

22. Ivey *et al*, *Physical oceanographic dynamics in the Kimberley*, WAMSI Kimberley Marine Research Project, No.2.2.1, December 2016, p.29.

23. Read, op.cit., 'Tides - Table 6.6', p.85.

REFERENCES

24. Garrow, op.cit., p.12.

25. Burns, R., *Tam o'Shanter*, Edinburgh Herald, James Sibbald, Scotland, 18 March 1791, Line 67.

26. Australian Heritage Council (AHC), 'Kimberley coastline: islands and reefs – a rich archipelago', in *Final Assessment of National Heritage Values of the West Kimberley: Description and History – One Place, Many Stories*, 2011, p.2.

27. Basedow, H., *Narrative of an Expedition of Exploration in North-Western Australia*, 2009, p.67.

28. National Geospatial - Intelligence Agency, op.cit.,'Approaches to King Sound – Sunday Strait', p.76.

29. ibid., p.76.

30. Zell, op.cit., 'Gaps', p.109.

31. Masefield, J., 'Sea Fever', in *Salt-Water Ballads*, 1902, pp.59-60.

CHAPTER 8: Unstable Atmospherics

1. Read, op. cit., p.123.

2. Guinness World Records, *Highest death toll caused by a hailstorm*, World Meteorological Organisation, May 2017, http://www.guinnessworldrecords.com/world-records/worst-hailstorm-disaster-death-toll. Accessed 15 February 2018.

3. Nalivkin, op.cit., 'Hail', p.314.

4. Ferrel, W.A., *Popular Treatise on the Winds*, 2nd Ed., p.432.

5. Henri, C., Insurance Council of Australia, 'The Sydney hailstorm: the insurance perspective', in *Australian Journal of Emergency Management*, vol.14. Issue 4, 2000. Archived from original 29 February 2008. Retrieved 15 February 2018, p.16.

6. Coenraadts, R., *Natural Disasters and How We Cope*, 2006, p.229.

7. United Nations' World Meteorological Organisation (WMO), *France*

strikes with longest-lasting lightning bolt, 16 September 2016.

https://phys.org/news/2016-09-france-longest-lasting-lightning.html. Retrieved 15 February 2018.

8. NASA Earth Observatory, *Global Lightning Activity*, 31 December 2013, https://earthobservatory.nasa.gov/IOTD/view.php?id=85600&eocn=image&eoci=moreiotd. Retrieved 16 February 2018.

9. Nalivkin, op.cit.,'Squall Storms' pp.174-75.

10. Bartlett, V., BBC Hampshire & Isle of Wight, *Haunted history of HMS Eurydice*, 28 October 2009, http://news.bbc.co.uk/local/hampshire/hi/people_and_places/history/newsid_8327000/8327961.stm. Accessed 16 February 2018.

11. Nalivkin, op.cit.,'Dust Storms', p.113.

12. ibid.

13. Egan, T., *The Worst Hard Time: The Untold Story Of Those Who Survived The Great American Dust Bowl*, 2006.

14. Nalivkin op.cit.,'Sandstorms', p.132-3.

15. ibid., p.133.

16. ibid.

17. ibid., 'Snowstorms', p.172.

18. ibid., 'Torrential Storms', p.196.

19. Averbuck, A. and Mc Carthy,C., 'Dumont d'Urville Station', in *Antarctica, Lonely Planet*, 5th Ed., p.120.

20. Gusev, A.M. (ed.), *The Novorossiiskaya bora* [Bora of Novorossiisk], in Tr. Morskogo Gidrofizicheskogo Instituta AN SSSR [Proceedings of the Marine Hydrophysical Institute], ASUSSR Publication, Moscow, vol.14, 1959 (in Russian), p.8.

21. Nalivkin, op.cit., 'Rain with Vertebrates', p.422.

22. Gudger, E.W., *More Rains of Fishes*, Annals and Magazine of Natural

REFERENCES

History, 10th series, vol.3, no.13, 1929, pp.1-26.

23. Nalivkin, op.cit., p.426.

CHAPTER 9: The Long Hike

1. Sigismund, F. F., 'The Happy Wanderer', 1850, Volksliedarchive, https://www.volksliederarchiv.de/mein-vater-war-ein-wandersmann/.

2. Stevens, K., 'Thru-Hikers', in *Freak Nation: A Field Guide to 101 of the MOST Odd, Extreme, and Outrageous American Subcultures*, 2010, p.143.

3. Hickman, M., 'Canada opens world's longest hiking trail that stretches coast to coast'. 6 September 2017, https://www.mnn.com/green-tech/transportation/blogs/canadas-great-trail-stretch-15000-miles-coast-coast. Retrieved 28 January 2018.

4. Wikipedia Encyclopedia, https://en.wikipedia.org/wiki/Continental_Divide_Trail, https://en.wikipedia.org/wiki/Pacific_Crest_Trail. Retrieved 28 January 2018.

5. North York Moors National Park Authority, "North York Moors National Park Facts and figures". Retrieved 4 March 2018.

6. Aalen, F., *The North East: English Heritage (England's Landscape)*, Vol.7, 2006.

7. Guinness World Records, 'World's longest stairs', Niesenbahn funicular railway, Spiez, Switzerland, www.guinnessworldrecords.com. Accessed 6 March 2018.

8. Sumitra, B., *Running Up 11,674 Steps in the World's Longest Single-Staircase Race*, Posted 14 October 2014, http://www.odditycentral.com/travel/running-up-11674-steps-in-the-worlds-longest-single-staircase-race.html. Retrieved 5 March 2018.

9. Fjord Norway, *Flørli Stairs and Rallarstien – Hike*, https://www.visitnorway.com/places-to-go/fjord-norway/the-stavanger-region/listings-stavanger/flørli-stairs-and-rallarstien-hike/185738/. 6 March 2018.

10. Demax (UK), 'Flørli stairs, Lysefjorden, Norway', in *Stairs: World's Longest Stairs*, https://www.demax.co.uk/worlds-longest-stairs/. Retrieved 5 March 2018.

11. Demax (UK), 'Potemkin Stairs, Odessa,Ukraine', in *Stairs: World's Longest Stairs*, Retrieved 5 March 2018.

12. Herlihy, P., *Odessa: A History*, 1794-1914, 1986, p.140.

13. Bell, M., 'Pailón del Diablo Waterfall, Ecuador', in *World's scariest stairs: Do you dare climb their steps?* Travel + Leisure. Posted 25 September 2014, https://edition.cnn.com/travel/article/worlds-scariest-stairs/index.html. Accessed 5 March 2018.

14. Lew, J., 'Pailon del Diablo, Ecuador', in *10 amazing outdoor staircases*, 23 February 2015, MNN Galleries. Accessed 5 March 2018.

15. Trifoni, J.,'Škraping in Dalmatia', in *The World's 100 Best Adventure Trips*, 2013, p.262.

16. Rogulj, D., 'Škraping in Pašman', 27 June 2016, *Adrenaline Croatia: 25 Things to Know about Adventure Tourism in Croatia*. Accessed 5 March 2018.

17. The Miroslav Krleža Institute of Lexicography, 'Adriatic Sea and islands', in *Croatia.eu – Land and people: Geography and population, Zagreb*, Croatia. Accessed 6 March 2018.

18. Magaš, D., 'The geographical situation and physical characteristics of island Pašman', in *Geographical position and basic natural-geographic features of the island of Pašman*, Croatian Geographical Bulletin, vol. 46, no.1, June 1984, p.71.

19. Mamut, M., *Geoecological evaluation of Island Pašman Relief Doc.* UDK 911.8:551.4 (497.581Pašman), Department of Geography, University of Zadar 14 July 2010, p.265.

20. Trifoni, op. cit., p. 262.

CHAPTER 10: Extreme Animals

1. Macdonald, D., (contributor/editor) and Norris, S.(ed.), *The New Ency-*

REFERENCES

clopedia of Mammals, 2001.

2. Australian Bilby Appreciation Society, *Save the Bilby Fund*, 2017. Retrieved 8 January 2018, https://savethebilbyfund.com/about-bilbies/biology.

3. ibid.

4. Australian Wildlife Preservation Society – *The Bilby*, https://www.aws.org.au/pdf/bilby/AWS_Project_Bilby.pdf. Retrieved 8 January 2018.

5. Debczak, M., *12 Wonderful Facts About Wombats*, 3 March 2016, http://mentalfloss.com/article/75981/12-wonderful-facts-about-wombats. Retrieved 8 January 2018.

6. Parker, S. P., (ed.), *Grzimek's Encyclopedia of Mammals*, vol 2, 1990, p.578.

7. Wikipedia Encyclopedia, 'Sloth', December 2017.

8. Gardner, A.L., 'Sloth, Mammal', in *Encyclopedia Brittanica*, 2018, https://www.britannica.com/animal/sloth. Accessed 8 January 2018.

9. Grzimeks, op.cit., p.597.

10. MacDonald, D., (ed.), *The Encyclopedia of Mammals*, part 1, 1984, p.41.

11. Conservation Institute, *10 fastest animals on earth – Cheetah*, 6 April 2014, http://www.conservationinstitute.org/10-fastest-animals-on-earth/. Retrieved 9 January 2018.

12. Hemstock, A., *The Polar Bear*, 1999, p.4.

13. Stirling, I., 'The First Polar Bears' in *Polar Bears*, 1988.

14. ibid.,'Behaviour'.

15. Pagano, A.M., Durner, G.M., Amstrup, S.C., Simac, K.S., and York, G.S., 'Long-distance swimming by polar bears (*Ursus maritimus*) of the southern Beaufort Sea during years of extensive open water', in *Canadian Journal Of Zoology*, vol. 90, 2012, pp.663-676.

16. Rosing, N., *The World of the Polar Bear*, 1996, pp.20-23.

17. Stirling, op.cit., 'Deadly Oceans', p.53.

18. Sea World, *Behavior -Polar Bears*, 2018, https://seaworld.org/en/animal-info/animal-infobooks/polar-bears/behavior. Retrieved 12 January 2018.

19. Australian Dog Lover Digital Magazine, *Australian Kelpie – Breed Profile*, July 2016, www.australiandoglover.com/2016/07/australian-kelpie-breed-profile.html. Retrieved 14 January 2018.

20. Collins Dictionary, *Australian Kelpie*, https://www.collinsdictionary.com/dictionary/english/kelpie

21. Wikipedia Encyclopedia, 'Platypus', December 2017, https://simple.wikipedia.org/wiki/Platypus.

22. National Geographic Society, 'Facts about Duck-Billed Platypus', images.nationalgeographic.com/wpf/sites/kids/NGS/wpf/printcreature/platypus.html. Retrieved 14 January 2018.

CHAPTER 11: Curious Avians

1. Coates, B.J., *The birds of Papua New Guinea, including the Bismarck Archipelago and Bougainville*, vol. 2, 1990, p.140.

2. Higgins, P.J., Peter, J.M. and Cowling, S.J., (eds.), Handbook of Australian, New Zealand and Antarctic Birds, vol. 7, part A: Boatbill to Larks, 2006, p.226.

3. Webb-Pullman, Bianca Z. and Elga, Mark A, 'The influence of time of day and environmental conditions on the foraging behaviours of willie wagtails, Rhipidura leucophrys', Department of Zoology, University of Melbourne, in *Australian Journal of Zoology*, vol 46, 1998, pp.137-144.

4. Coates, op.cit.

5. BirdLife Australia and The Guardian newspaper, December 2017, https://www.bhg.com.au ›Home›News›Magpie crowned Australian Bird of the Year. Accessed 3 January 2018.

6. National Geographic Society, 'Animals - Blue-Footed Booby', in *National Geographic, https://www.nationalgeographic.com/animals/birds/b/*

REFERENCES

blue-footed-booby/. Retrieved 4 January 2018.

7. Wikipedia Encyclopedia, 'Blue-footed booby', Accessed 4 January 2018.

8. National Geographic, op.cit., 'Blue-Footed Booby'.

9. Del Hoyo, J., Elliott, A., and Sargatal, J., (eds.), ' Sulidae –gannets and boobies' in *Handbook of the Birds of the World*, vol.1: *Ostrich to Ducks*, Lynx Edicions, Spain, 1992.

10. Wikipedia Encyclopedia, 'Guatemala', in *List of National Birds*, December 2017, https://en.wikipedia.org/wiki/List_of_national_birds . Accessed 3 January 2018.

11. National Geographic Society, 'Animals -Resplendent Quetzal', in National Geographic, https://www.nationalgeographic.com/animals/birds/r/resplendent-quetzal. Accessed 3 January 2018.

12. National Aviary, 'Rhinoceros Hornbill', in *The National Aviary Website*, https://www.aviary.org/animals/rhinoceros-hornbill. Retrieved 3 January 2018.

13. Long, M., 'Hornbills, Their Nest-Building Behavior and Species in Asia', in *Facts and Details*, November 2012, factsanddetails.com/asian/cat68/sub435/item2430.html. January 2018.

14. Terres, J. K., *The Audubon Society Encyclopedia of North American Birds*, 1980. p. 959.

15. Houston, D.C., "Family Cathartidae (New World vultures)", in *Handbook of the Birds of the World, Volume 2: New World Vultures to Guineafowl*, 1994, pp. 24–41.

16. Ferguson-Lees, J. and Christie, D. A., *Raptors of the World*, 2001, pp. 88, 315–16.

17. Higgins, P. J., Peter, J.M. and Cowling, S. J. (eds.), *Handbook of Australian, New Zealand and Antarctic Birds*, vol. 7, part B: Dunnock to Starlings, 2006, p.1290.

CHAPTER 12: Fearsome Swimmers

1. Knickle, C., 'Tiger Shark', Ichthyology Collection, Florida Museum of Natural History, University of Florida, USA, https://www.floridamuseum.ufl.edu/fish/discover/species-profiles/galeocerdo-cuvier. Retrieved 22 February 2018.

2. Harvey, D., *Super Shark Encyclopedia And Other Creatures Of The Deep*, 2015, p.173-5.

3. ibid., p.36.

4. Taylor, L. R.,*The Sharks of Hawaii: Their Biology and Cultural Significance*, 1993.

5. Dr.Ritter, E. K.,'Fact Sheet: Tiger Sharks', *Shark Info – Research News and Background Information on the Protection, Ecology, Biology and Behavior of Sharks*, Updated 4 June 2016, http://www.sharkinfo.ch/SI4_99e/gcuvier.html. Accessed 23 February 2018.

6. Bester, C., 'Great barracuda', Ichthyology Collection, Florida Museum of Natural History, University of Florida, USA, https://www.floridamuseum.ufl.edu/fish/discover/species-profiles/sphyraena-barracuda.

7. Grubich, J. R., Huskey, S., Crofts,S., Orti, G.,and Porto,J., *"Mega-Bites: Extreme jaw forces of living and extinct piranhas (Serrasalmidae)"*. Scientific Reports 2, Article 1009, 20 December 2012, doi:10.1038/srep01009, Nature Publishing Group. Accessed 25 February 2018.

8. BBC News Online, 2 July 2007. *"Piranha 'less deadly than feared'"*. Science and Environment, Retrieved 25 February 2018.

9. Berkovitz, B.K.B., and Shellis, R.P., 'A longitudinal study of tooth succession in piranhas (Pisces: Characidae), with an analysis of the tooth replacement cycle', in *Journal of Zoology*, Vol. 184, Issue 4, DOI: 10.1111/j.1469-7998.1978.tb03306.x, London, April 1978, pp.545-61.

10. Freeman,B., Nico,L.G., Osentoksi, M., Jelks, H.L., and Collins, T.M., 'Molecular systematics of Serrasalmidae:Deciphering the identities of piranha species and unravelling their evolutionary histories', in *Zootaxa* 1484, Online Edition, Magnolia Press, 28 May 2007, http://www.mapress.

REFERENCES

com/zootaxa/2007f/zt01484p038.pdf, p.1.

11. Hubert, N., Duponchelle, F., Nuñez, J., Garcia-Davila, C., Paugy, D., Renno, J.F., 'Phylogeography of the piranha genera *Serrasalmus* and *Pygocentrus*:implications for the diversification of the Neotropical ichthyfauna', in *Molecular Ecology, Vol.16, Issue10*, DOI: 10.1111/j.1365-294X.2007.03267.x, May 2007, p.1.

12. Lieske, E. and Myers, R., *Collins Pocket Guide - Coral reef fishes. Indo-Pacific & Caribbean including the Red Sea.* 1st Ed., 1994.

13. Robertson-Browne, N., and Robertson-Browne, C., *Deadly Oceans – In Search Of The Deadliest Sea Creatures*, 2016, pp.136-45.

14. Harvey, op.cit.,'Giant Moray Eel', pp.14-15.

15. Robertson-Browne, op.cit., pp.168-71.

16. Heatwole, H., *Sea Snakes, Australian Natural History Series*, 1999, p.118, p.126.

17. ibid., pp. 118-19.

18. ibid., p.121.

19. Rasmussen, A., Sanders, K., Lobo, A. & Courtney, T., 'Enhydrina schistosa', in *The IUCN (International Union for Conservation of Nature and Natural Resources) Red List of Threatened Species*, 2010: e. T176719A7289781.

20. Heatwole, op.cit., Plate 14, p.53.

CHAPTER 13: Festivals and Other Extremes

1. Shakespeare, W., 'All the world's a stage', in *As You Like It*, Act II, Scene VII, *Mr William Shakespeares Comedies*, Histories, & Tragedies, London, 1623, p.185.

2. Bryson, L., 'This Tiny Beach Town Hosts an Enormous Clown Parade Each Year', *Fodor's Travel Guide*, Posted 5 February 2018, https://www.fodors.com/news/author/lucy-bryson. Retrieved 8 March 2018.

3. ibid.

4. Stevens, K., 'Clowns', in *Freak Nation: A Field Guide to 101 of the MOST Odd, Extreme, and Outrageous American Subcultures*, 2010, p.163.

5. Housel, D., 'Jesters of Old, Clowns of Today', in *Read and Succeed Comprehension Level 4: Paraphrasing Passages and Questions*, #50727, 2010, p.125.

6. ibid.

7. Steinhauser, G., 'Holi Festivals Spread Far From India', *The Wall Street Journal*, issue 3 October 2013, Accessed 12 March 2018.

8. Jones, C., 'Holi', in *Religious Celebrations: An Encyclopedia of Holidays, Festivals, Solemn Observances, and Spiritual Commemorations*, Melton, J.G. (ed.), vol.1, 2011.

9. Williams, V., 'Adolescence and Early Adulthood', in *Celebrating Life Customs around the World: From Baby Showers to Funerals*, vol. 2, 2016, p.75.

10. Shetland Islands Council, 2012, http://www.shetland.gov.uk/. Retrieved 13 March 2018.

11. Schei, L.K., *The Shetland Isles*, 2006, pp. 11-12.

12. Jamieson, T.,'A Very Brief History of Up-Helly-Aa', Shetland Library, www.shetland-library.gov.uk/documents/AVeryBriefHistoryofUp_000.pdf. Accessed 13 March 2018.

13. Oliver, N., *Vikings: A History*, 2012, p.9.

14. Andrews, S., 'Up Helly Aa: a Scottish festival where people dress up like Vikings and set fire to a longship', in *The Vintage News*, 4 December 2017, www.thevintagenews.com/2017/12/04/up-helly-aa/.

15. ibid.

16. Erulski,I., and Notteva,S., Pernik Regional History Museum, 'They gathered in a book everything about the name of Pernik': Article by Borisova, Rumi, 21 October 2014, http://gradski.org/archives/46163.

17. Davey, op.cit., 'Apokreas – Galaxidi', p.203, pp.231-32.

REFERENCES

18. SPIEGAL ONLINE, *The Flour Wars of Galaxidi*, 19 August 2008, http://www.spiegel.de/international/europe/farinaceous-food-fight-the-flour-wars-of-galaxidi-a-572974.html, Retrieved 27 March 2018.

19. Bicanski, M., Full Frame –Flour Wars, *GlobalPost*, 30 May 2010. Accessed 27 March 2018.

20. SPIEGAL ONLINE, op.cit.,*The Flour Wars of Galaxidi*.

21. Davey, S., 'Stavelot Carnival', in *Around The World In 500 Festivals: From Burning Man in the US to Kumbh Mela in Allahabad –The World's Most Spectacular Celebrations*, 2016, p.198.

22. Royal Comité des Fêtes, Laetare of Stavelot – A Little History, http://www.laetare-stavelot.be/laetare/peu-dhistoire/. Accessed 17 March 2018.

23. Thunus, O., 'Carnival: Laetare de Stavelot will completely change course', https://www.rtbf.be/info/regions/liege/detail_carnaval-le-laetare-de-stavelot-va-completement-changer-de-parcours?id=9513863, 27 January 2017. Accessed 17 March 2018.

24. Davey, op.cit.,'Bizarre Britain - Wales', p.251.

25. Guinness World Records, 'Fastest time to complete Women's World Bog Snorkelling', 24 August 2014, www.guinnessworldrecords.com/world-records/fastest-time-to-complete-women's-world-bog-snorkelling. Retrieved 17 March 2018.

26. O'Shea, B, 'Coogee Jetty to Jetty Swim's unlucky duck Daphne missing off WA Coast', in *The West Australian*, Inside Cover, West Australian Newspapers Limited, Perth, Australia, Issue 16 March 2018, p.2.

27. Megson, M., 'Bad Luck Rubber Duck', in *The Bookworm's Brain – Funny Poems for Children: A collection of 42 funny poems and illustrations*, 30 July 2011.

28. Hofman, F., *Canard de Bain St. Nazaire*, 2007, florentijnhofman.nl. Accessed 19 March 2018.

29. Gornall, J., 'Newsmaker: The rubber duck, Lifestyle section' in *The National*, issue 5 December 2013, https://www.thenational.ae/lifestyle/newsmaker-the-rubber-duck-1.323045. Accessed 19 March 2018.

30. Hohn, D., *Moby~Duck: The True Story of 28,800 Bath Toys Lost at Sea*, February 2012.

CHAPTER 14: Neon Technodreams

1. Ribbat, C., 'Reading Neon', in *Flickering Light: A History of Neon*, 2013, p.7.

2. Hess, A., *Viva Las Vegas: After-Hours Architecture*, 1993, p.74.

3. Moreno, R., *Nevada Curiosities: Quirky Characters, Roadside Oddities & Other Offbeat Stuff*, 1st Ed., 2008, p.1880.

4. The Neon Group, 'Knowledge Center', in *Brighter Thinking*, 2017, http://www.theneongroup.org/knowledge.html, Accessed 21 March 2018.

5. Ribbat, op,cit., 'Green Fingers', p.118.

6. Stern, 'Sculpture; Sun Sign', in *Contemporary Neon*, 1990, p.135.

7. ibid.,'Sculpture; The Fire Dance (Frederica Marangoni, 1988)', p.155.

8. ibid., p.100.

9. ibid., 'Sculpture; Electro Man', p.177.

10. Sprengnagel, D. J., *Neon World*, 1999, p.126.

11. Searich, *Neon Light*, April 2012, https://hellopoetry.com/searich/.

12. Glow Inc., *Black Light -Technical information*, 2010, Archived from the original on 29 June 2013, Retrieved 23 March 2018.

13. Juicy Body Art, 'What's a blacklight? in *UV Blacklight Parties –What You Need To Know To Glow*, Melbourne, Australia, http://www.juicy-bodyart.com/uv-black-light-parties-what-you-need-to-know-to-glow/#.WrhEAkxuLIU, Accessed 26 March 2018.

14. Hilliard, R., The Top 10 Music Festivals in the World, 18 June 2012, http://festivalfling.com/best-music-festivals-2012/, Accessed 26 March 2018.

CHAPTER 15: Footbridges and Gnomes

REFERENCES

1. Quotes and Quotations of Mehmet Murat ildan #26, 5 February 2013, https://muratildanquotations.wordpress.com/category/quotations/page/5/, Retrieved 31 March 2018.

2. ibid., #12, 10 March 2011, https://muratildanquotations.wordpress.com/category/quotations/page/7/, Retrieved 31 March 2018.

3. Longfellow, H., *The Belfry of Bruges and Other Poems*, 1st Ed., 1846, pp.61-2.

4. Zermatt Tourism, *The Longest Suspension Bridge in the World is Open*, 29 July 2017, https://www.zermatt.ch/en/Media/Media-corner/Press-releases/The-Longest-Suspension-Bridge-in-the-World-is-Open, Retrieved 6 April 2018.

5. Briggs, K.M., *The Fairies in Tradition and Literature*, 2nd Ed., 1967, p.208.

6. Briggs, K.M., *A Dictionary of Fairies: Hobgoblins, Brownies, Bogies and Other Supernatural Creatures*, 1976, p.193.

7. Huygen, W., 'Physical Appearance- The Cap', in *The Complete Gnomes*, 1994.

8. ibid., 'The Gnome and the Weather'.

9. Mill, J.S., 'Chapter 3: Of Individuality, as one of the Elements of Well-Being', in *On Liberty*, 1859, p.83.

10. Thorne, D., Guinness World Records, 'Largest collection of gnomes and pixies', 15 August 2015, http://www.guinnessworldrecords.com/news/60at60/2015/8/2000-largest-collection-of-garden-gnomes-392875, Retrieved 17 April 2018.

11. Butler, M., 'News -Who started WA's attraction Gnomesville?', in *The West Australian*, Issue 4 December 2017, https://thewest.com.au/news/wa/who-started-was-attraction-gnomesville-ng-b88661417z, Retrieved 29 March 2018.

12. ibid.

13. O'Shea, B.,'Inside Cover –Gnomes Today', in *The West Australian*, Issue 31 March 2018, p.2.

14. Glyde, C., 'Secret Aussie Road Trips Stops:Out-of-the-way attractions for smaller crowds and quirkier adventures – Gnomesville', in *Departures* Magazine, Journal International Experience GmbH, American Express Services Europe, London, June 2014. https://departures-international.com/travel/.../pacific/australia/road-trip-stops-australia.

15. Geers, L and Forrest, C. (ed.), *Gnomesville: The Real Story*, 2017, p.38.

16. House and Home, 'Fun Facts: 10 things you need to know about Garden Gnomes', Posted 14 June 2012, https://www.houseandhome.ie/news-events/fun-facts-10-things-you-need-know-about-garden-gnomes-1686, Retrieved 19 April 2018.

CHAPTER 16 Over the Edge

1. Thompson, H.S., *Hell's Angels: The Strange and Terrible Saga of the Outlaw Motorcycle Gangs*, 1966.

2. McGough, R., 'Not for Me a Youngman's Death', in *As Far As I Know*, 2012.

3. Aurelius Augustinus, Saint Augustine, Bishop of Hippo, 396- 430 AD.

4. Boroson, M.H., *The Girl with Ghost Eyes*, 2015, p.27.

BIBLIOGRAPHY

Aalen, Fred, *The North East: English Heritage (England's Landscape)*, vol.7, Collins, 2006.

Annals and Magazine of Natural History, 10th series, vol.3, no.13, Taylor and Francis Ltd., London, 1929.

Astley, Neil (ed.), *Funny Ha-Ha, Funny Peculiar: A Book of Strange & Comic Poems*, Bloodaxe Books, Northumberland, England, 2015.

Australian Government Attorney-General's Department, *Australian Journal of Emergency Management*, vol.14. issue 4, Summer 1999-2000, Emergency Management Australia, Mount Macedon, Victoria, 2000.

Australian Heritage Council (AHC), *Final Assessment of National Heritage Values of the West Kimberley: Description and History – One Place, Many Stories*, Australian Government Press, Canberra, 2011.

Averbuck, Alexis, *Antarctica, Lonely Planet*, 5th Ed., Lonely Planet Publications November 2012.

Basedow, Herbert, *Narrative of an Expedition of Exploration in North-West-*

ern Australia, Hesperian Press, Perth, Australia, 2009.

Boroson, M.H., *The Girl with Ghost Eyes: The Daoshi Chronicles (Book One)*, Talos Press, New York, USA, 2015.

Briggs, Katherine Mary, *The Fairies in Tradition and Literature*, 2nd Ed., Routledge and Kegan Paul, London, 1967.

Briggs, Katherine Mary, *A Dictionary of Fairies: Hobgoblins, Brownies, Bogies and Other Supernatural Creatures*, Allen Lane, London, 1976.

Canadian Journal Of Zoology, vol 90, NRC Research Press, https://doi.org/10.1139/z2012-033, 2012.

Carus, Paul (ed.), *The Open Court: Devoted to the Science of Religion, the, Religion of Science, and the Extension of the Religious Parliament Idea*, vol.17, no.8, The Open Court Publishing Company, Chicago, Illinois, USA, August 1903.

Coates, Brian J., *The birds of Papua New Guinea, including the Bismarck Archipelago and Bougainville*, vol 2, Dove Publications, Alderley Queensland, 1990.

Coenraadts, Robert Raymond, *Natural Disasters and How We Cope*, The Five Mile Press, Victoria, Australia, 2006.

Cooper, Paul (ed.), *Australian Journal of Zoology*, vol. 46, CSIRO Publishing, Collingwood, Victoria, 1998.

Croatian Geographic Society, *Croatian Geographical Bulletin*, vol. 46, no.1, Zagreb, June 1984.

Davey, Steve, *Around The World In 500 Festivals: From Burning Man in the US to Kumbh Mela in Allahabad –The World's Most Spectacular Celebrations*, Skyhorse Publishing, New York, USA, 2016.

Del Hoyo, Josep, Elliott, Andrew, and Sargatal, Jordi., (eds.), *Handbook of the Birds of the World*, vol.1: Ostrich to Ducks, Lynx Edicions, Barcelona, Spain, 1992.

Del Hoyo, Josep, Elliott, Andrew, and Sargatal, Jordi., (eds.), *Handbook of the Birds of the World,* vol. 2: *New World Vultures to Guineafowl*, Lynx Edicions, Barcelona, Spain, 1994.

Egan, Timothy, *The Worst Hard Time: The Untold Story Of Those Who Survived The Great American Dust Bowl*, Houghton Mifflin, New York, 2006.

Ferguson-Lees, James and Christie, David A., *Raptors of the World*, Houghton Mifflin Company, New York, USA, 2001.

Ferrel, William, *Popular Treatise on the Winds*, 2nd Ed., New York, 1890.

Flood, Brian, and Papenhausen, Richard (ed.), *Saint John: A Sporting Tradition 1785-1985*, Neptune Publishing, New Brunswick, Canada, 1985.

Garrow, S. C., *Big tide country: a book about the Kimberley's tides and tidal life*, Self published, Brighton, Victoria, Australia, 2002.

Geers, Lesley and Forrest, Carmel (ed.), *Gnomesville: The Real Story*, Ferguson Valley Marketing and Promotion Inc., Eaton, Western Australia, 2017.

Hapgood, Alex, *Kiteboarding: Where It's At ...*, Adlard Coles Nautical/Bloomsbury, London, 2014.

Harvey, Derek, *Super Shark Encyclopedia And Other Creatures Of The Deep*, Dorling Kindersley Publishing, New York, USA, 2015.

Heathcote, John Moyer, and Tebbutt, Charles Goodman, *Skating*, Longmans, Green and Company, London, 1892.

Heatwole, Harold, *Sea Snakes, Australian Natural History Series*, UNSW Press, Sydney, Australia, 1999.

Heller, Peter, *Hell Or High Water: Surviving Tibet's Tsongpo River*, Allen and Unwin, Sydney, 2014.

Hemstock, Annie, *The Polar Bear*, Capstone Press, Manakato, MN, USA 1999.

Herlihy, Patricia, *Odessa: A History, 1794-1914*. Harvard University Press,

Cambridge, MA, USA, 1986.

Hess, Alan, *Viva Las Vegas: After-Hours Architecture*, Chronicle Books, San Francisco, 1993.

Hicks, Kelli, *Hot Air Ballooning*, Britannica Digital Learning, London, 2013.

Higgins, Peter Jeffrey, Peter, John M., and Cowling, S. J. (eds.), *Handbook of Australian, New Zealand and Antarctic Birds*, vol. 7, part A: Boatbill to Larks, Oxford University Press, Melbourne, 2006.

Higgins, Peter Jeffrey, Peter, John M., Cowling S. J. (eds.), *Handbook of Australian, New Zealand and Antarctic Birds*, vol. 7, part B: Dunnock to Starlings, Oxford University Press, Melbourne, 2006.

Hill, Dean, *Snowboarding: The Fundamentals And Beyond*, New Holland Publishers, Sydney, Australia, 2001.

Hohn, Donovan, *Moby~Duck: The True Story of 28,800 Bath Toys Lost at Sea*, Union Books, United Kingdom, February 2012.

Housel, Debra, *Read and Succeed Comprehension Level 4: Paraphrasing Passages and Questions*, #50727, Shell Education, California, USA, 2010.

Howell, Sara, and Saxena, Shalini (ed.), *Whirlpools*, Britannica Educational Publishing, Chicago, Illinois, USA, 2017.

Huygen, Wil, *The Complete Gnomes*, H.N.Abrams, New York, 1994.

Ivey, Greg, Brinkman, Richard, Lowe, Ryan, Jones, Nicole, Symonds, Graham, and Espinosa-Gayosso, Alexis, *Physical oceanographic dynamics in the Kimberley*, Report of Project 2.2.1 prepared for the Kimberley Marine Research Program, Western Australian Marine Science Institution, Perth, Western Australia, 2016.

Kotar, A.L and Gessler J.E. (ed.), *Ballooning: A History*, 1792-1900, McFarland & Company, Jefferson, North Carolina and London, 2014.

Labrecque, Ellen, *Cliff Diving*, The Child's World, Mankato, Minnesota, USA, 2012.

BIBLIOGRAPHY

Leden, Judy, *Flying with Condors,* Orion Books. New York, 2003.

Lieske, Ewald and Myers, Robert, *Collins Pocket Guide - Coral reef fishes. Indo-Pacific & Caribbean including the Red Sea*, 1st Ed., Harper Collins Publishers, United Kingdom,1994.

Longfellow, Henry, *The Belfry of Bruges and Other Poems*, 1st Ed., John Owen, Cambridge, 1846.

MacDonald, David (ed.), *The Encyclopedia of Mammals*, part 1, Allen & Unwin, Sydney, 1984.

Macdonald, David and Norris, Sasha, *The New Encyclopedia of Mammals*. Oxford University Press, Oxford, 2001.

McCormick, Elizabeth Wilde, *Living on the Edge:Breaking Through Instead of Breaking Down*, Element Books Limited, Great Britain, USA, Australia, 1997.

McGough, Roger, *As Far As I Know*, Penguin Books, London, UK, 2012.

Masefield, John, *Salt-Water Ballads*, Grant Richards, London, 1902.

Marcus, Benjamin, *Extreme Surf*, Pavilion Books, London, 2008.

Maxwell, Kerry, *Brave New Words: A Language Lover's Guide to the 21st Century*, Macmillan Press, London, 2006.

Megson, Mark, *The Bookworm's Brain – Funny Poems for Children: A collection of 42 funny poems and illustrations*, Self published, United Kingdom, 30 July 2011.

Melton, J.Gordon (ed.), with Beverley, James, Buck, Christopher, Jones and Constance, *Religious Celebrations: An Encyclopedia of Holidays, Festivals, Solemn Observances, and Spiritual Commemorations*, vol.1, ABC-CLIO, Califormia, Colorado and Oxford, 2011.

Mill, John Stuart, *On Liberty*, Oxford University Press, London, 1859.

Moreno, Richard, *Nevada Curiosities: Quirky Characters, Roadside Oddities & Other Offbeat Stuff*, 1st Ed., Globe Pequot Press, Connecticut, USA,

2008.

Nalivkin, Dmitrii Vasilevich, V.V. Bhattacharya (Translator), V.S. Kothekar (ed.), *Hurricanes, storms and tornadoes: Geographic characteristics and geological activity*, A.A. Balkema, Rotterdam, 1983.

National Geospatial - Intelligence Agency, *Sailing Directions (Enroute) North, West, and South Coasts of Australia*, Publication 175, 12th Ed., Springfield, Virginia, USA, 2014.

Nestor, James, *Deep: Freediving, Renegade Science, and What The Ocean Tells Us About Ourselves*, Profile Books, London, 2014.

Oliver, Neil, *Vikings: A History*, Weidenfeld & Nicolson, London, 2012.

Parker, Sybil P., (ed.), *Grzimek's Encyclopedia of Mammals*, vol 2, McGraw-Hill, New York, 1990.

Raymo, Chet, *The Soul of the Night – An Astronomical Pilgrimage*, Prentice Hall Press, New Jersey, USA, 1985.

Read, Ian, *Continent of Extremes: Recording Australia's Natural Phenomena*, UNSW Press, Sydney, Australia, 1998.

Ribbat, Christoph, *Flickering Light: A History of Neon,* Reaktion Books Ltd, London, 2013.

Roberts, William and Bull, R. Charles, *Bull's Handbook of Sports Injuries*, 2nd Ed., McGraw-Hill, Europe, 2004.

Robertson-Browne, Nick, and Robertson-Browne, Caroline, *Deadly Oceans – In Search Of The Deadliest Sea Creatures*, Reed New Holland Publishing, London, Sydney and Auckland, 2016.

Rosing, Norbert, *The World of the Polar Bear*, Firefly Books Ltd, Willowdale, Ontario, 1996.

Ryan, Kalya, *50 Festivals to Blow Your Mind* (Lonely Planet), Lonely Planet Global Limited May 2017.

Sagert, Kelly Boyer, *Encyclopedia of Extreme Sport*, Greenwood Press,

Connecticut and London, 2009.

Schei, Liv Kjorsvik, *The Shetland Isles*, Colin Baxter Photography, Grantown-on-Spey, 2006.

Scott, A.W. (Sandy), *A Traveller's Guide: Kimberley Coast: Bays, Basins, Islands and Estuaries*, Envirobook, Sussex Inlet, NSW, 2012.

Scott, Ridley, (Dir.), *Blade Runner*, Sci-Fi Film, Warner Brothers, 1982.

Seura, Suomalaisen Kirjallisuuden and Bosley, Keith (translator and editor), *Skating on the Sea: Poetry from Finland*, Finnish Literature Society/Bloodaxe Books Ltd, Helsinki, Finland and Newcastle-on-Tyne, 1997.

Smith, Phoebe, *Wild Nights:Camping Britain's Extremes*, Summersdale Publishers, Chichester, West Sussex, UK, 2015.

Sprengnagel, Dusty, *Neon World*, Harper Collins, New York, 1999.

Stern, Rudi, *Contemporary Neon*, Retail Reporting Corporation, New York, USA, 1990.

Stevens, Kate, *Freak Nation: A Field Guide to 101 of the MOST Odd, Extreme, and Outrageous American Subcultures*, Adams Media, MA, USA, 2010.

Stirling, Ian, *Polar Bears*, University of Michigan Press, Ann Arbor, USA, 1988.

Szilagyi, Wade, *CMOS Bulletin SCMO*, vol.31, no.6, Canadian Meteorological and Oceanographic Society, Ontario, Canada, December 2003.

Taylor, Leighton R., *The Sharks of Hawaii: Their Biology and Cultural Significance*, University of Hawaii Press, Honolulu, 1993.

Terres, John Kenneth, T*he Audubon Society Encyclopedia of North American Birds*, Knopf, New York, USA, 1980.

The West Australian newspaper, Issue 4 December 2017, West Australian Newspapers Limited, Perth, Australia, 2017.

The West Australian newspaper, Issue 31 March 2018, West Australian

Newspapers Limited, Perth, Australia, 2018.

Thompson, Hunter, S., *Hell's Angels: The Strange and Terrible Saga of the Outlaw Motorcycle Gangs*, Random House, New York, USA, 1966.

Trifoni, Jasmina, *The World's 100 Best Adventure Trips*, White Star Publishers, Novara, Italy, 2013.

Waring, Rob (ed.), *Extreme Skydiving*, National Geographic, Heinle Cengage Learning, London, 2010.

Watkins-Pitchford, Denys ("BB"), *The Little Grey Men*, 1st Ed., Eyre & Spottiswoode, London, 1942.

Whiting, Ken, and Varette, Kevin, *Whitewater Kayaking: The Ultimate Guide*, 2nd Ed, Helconia Press, East Petersburg, Pennsylvania, USA, 2012.

Williams, Victoria, *Celebrating Life Customs around the World: From Baby Showers to Funerals*, vol. 2, ABC-CLIO, Califormia and Colorado, 2016.

Yeung, Yue-man, and Shen, Jianfa, (eds.), *Developing China's West: A Critical Path to Balanced National Development*, Chinese University Press, Hong Kong, 2004.

Zell, Len, *Kimberley Coast: A guide to the Kimberley Coast wilderness: north-western Western Australia*, 2nd Ed., Wild Discovery, Armidale, Australia, 2007.

ABOUT THE AUTHOR

Figure 46: Start of the Adventure (© Shutterstock)

Simon King is an emerging Australian author who has already published four books: *Crocodiles and Cocktails* (Hesperian Press, 2017), *Witchcraft, Whispers, Shadows and Strange Sights*, and *Marbles, Marella Jubes and Milk Bottles* and *Robot Awakening* (Conscious Care Publishing, 2017-2018). Each book encompasses different aspects of life's journey, and engages many interesting historical and contemporary perspectives.

ON THE EDGE

This book embraces the challenging subject of extreme sports, leisure pursuits, celebratory festivals, climatic and elemental phenomena, as well as the many unusual species of fauna that inhabit our planet.

The quirky and the bizarre have always fascinated the author, and so have been integrated into this book in recognition of what it truly means to experience extreme life, whether that be through various personal interests, recreational pursuits or by simply enjoying the fascination of the strange.

www.ingramcontent.com/pod-product-compliance
Lightning Source LLC
Chambersburg PA
CBHW071924290426
44110CB00013B/1466